D1232975

DEP-ANON

A 12 Step Recovery Program for Families and Friends of the Depressed

For group discussions and personal enrichment

Depressed Anonymous Publications
P.O. Box 465
Pewee Valley Kentucky 40056

DEP-ANON © 2021
Depressed Anonymous Publications

Web site http://www.depressedanon.com
Email depanon@netpenny.net

ISBN 978-1-929438-19-8

DEDICATION

DEP-ANON -is dedicated to all the families and friends of the depressed whose lives are very much a part of the life of their depressed loved one. We believe that DEP-ANON, a Twelve Step recovery program, will be a formidable resource to be shared in a DEP-ANON fellowship setting.

AUTHOR'S ACKNOWLEDGEMENTS

I want to thank my friends Charley and Mary Ellen with Bob Garvey of Louisville, Kentucky. They encouraged me to write Dep-Anon, a Twelve Step recovery program for families and friends of the depressed.

I thank Mr. David Fields of Fields Computer Services for his commitment to Depressed Anonymous Publications, providing hope to the depressed and their family members. He continues to get the word out of who we are and what we do through our books and literature.

I am grateful to Judith Rice, a member of the Ursuline Sisters of Louisville, Kentucky, for her time and energy spent proofreading and editing the Dep-Anon manuscript.

To my wife, Diane Margaret Smith, for her continued support for our work with persons depressed and their families.

I am grateful for those who have been depressed and part of our own families who give those who still suffer from depression the belief that they too can recover.

Contents

DEDICATION 3

AUTHOR'S ACKNOWLEDGEMENTS 4

INTRODUCTION 6

SECTION ONE

DEP-ANON PROVIDES HELP FOR FAMILY MEMBERS OF THE
DEPRESSED 12

GEARING UP FOR ACTION 19

THE BIRTH OF DEP-ANON TO THY SELF BED TRUE 26

BEING PART OF THE CONVERSATION: A COLLABORATIVE MODEL.. 34

DEP-ANON FAMILY GROUP: A HEALTHY CONNECTION BETWEEN THE
DEPRESSED AND THE FAMILY 42

SECTION TWO

WHAT IS DEPRESSION? 49

FAMILY SELF-CARE. WHERE DO WE START? 59

LIVING IN THE SOLUTION.. 66

DEP-ANON IS OUR NORTH STAR! 72

SUPPORT OF THE FAMILY IS ESSENTIAL 77

DO WE HAVE A "CURE" MENTALITY? 86

THE IMPORTANCE OF BELONGING TO A MUTUAL AID GROUP 94

APPENDIX A.. 99

APPENDIX B.. 101

APPENDIX C.. 104

APPENDIX D 112

BIBLIOGRAPHY 117

INTRODUCTION

Tradition Five of the DEP-ANON Family Group

"Each DEP-ANON group has but one purpose, to help families of the depressed. We do this by practicing the Twelve Steps ourselves, encouraging and understanding our depressed family member, and welcoming and giving comfort to families and friends of the depressed."

DEP-ANON is a support group for the family and friends of the depressed. This recovery program is much like Al-Anon, promoting health and healing for the family and friends of the depressed. We do this by focusing on ourselves, using all the tools for maintaining our spiritual, emotional, mental, and physical health.

Over the years, I continue my work with the depressed and with the families and friends of the depressed. I see a great need to offer help for the depressed and their families. Many people do not have an accurate understanding of the nature of depression with its debilitating and isolating effect upon the human mind and physical wellness of the depressed.

In 1985 I launched the Twelve Step Depressed Anonymous recovery program for those men and women who suffer from depression. The depressed person is no longer alone but surrounded by their peers in the Depressed Anonymous fellowship. The members of this fellowship understand depression, finding recovery together. My **"pressing concern"** as a therapist and fellow human providing family members with the help they need to support each other. I am now making available the manual DEP-ANON, a resource and essential guide for the families and friends of the depressed. They will now have their recovery program based on the Twelve Steps and gain a critical understanding of depression. They will have "new eyes" to see the true nature of the depression experienced as lived out in the lives of their DSO. Not only will their attitudes change, so will their relationship with those who are depressed.

We will learn that we cannot change anyone but ourselves. Our spiritual principles of the 12 Steps will provide us with a spiritual power we recognize as more prominent than ourselves. And we will invest in this power, promoting a faith that will keep our focus on ourselves and not the futility of our trying to "fix" them.

It is essential to shift our attention to our self-care, ensuring that we meet our mental health and emotional needs. More significant than ourselves, it continues to bring family and friends together, strengthening our bonds with each other. We each continue to emphasize our recovery as we become less inclined to place our trust in ourselves alone. Now we can put our trust in our mutual efforts in taking care of our spiritual needs and not consumed by our DSO's needs. We are no longer alone. We will be facing challenging times, and we will not fail ourselves or our fellowship. We will understand that we didn't cause the depression. We will comprehend that we cannot control their depression, behavior, or thinking. We also will learn that we cannot "cure" their depression. What we can do is live out our recovery program, keeping the focus on our own mental, spiritual, and emotional wellbeing. As you will see, we are combining each chapter of our work with an individual Step with its commentary and questions. These commentaries and questions will provide you with your reflections as possible topics for group discussions.

This DEP-ANON manual divided into TWO SECTIONS, each with its emphasis. Section One concerns the need for the family group DEP-ANON, which includes a depressed member as part of their family. Section Two acquaints us with the nature of depression and how it affects the lives of those who experience it.

SECTION ONE

When we examine our own lives, we discover that our DSO, like ourselves, is looking for a plan that works. Due to putting the Steps to work in our own lives, some of us have already experienced the power of the Twelve Steps. In this respect, we believe that we have the promises that our own lives will change for the better. Both the DSO and our DEP-ANON Family group have come to believe that a power greater than ourselves will and can restore us to sanity, bringing a new healthy way to relate to each other.

Now let's get on with our self-care and begin that adventure with others like ourselves. DEP-ANON can be a powerful experience for strengthening each of us as we help each other. We happen to all be on the same page. We are discovering that the best care for others is to first take care of ourselves. We learn that we must live in the solution, live for the "what is possible," and not live with the pessimism and attitudes with our DSO that make matters worse and not better. (See Appendix A) We will keep our focus on ourselves and gradually put into practice the skills, boundaries, and actions that can continue to solidify our efforts to maintain our mental wellness and a balanced family life

SECTION ONE: The Chapter headings and submenus are listed here in the order of their occurrence.
Chapter 1) Dep-Anon is Help for Family Members of the Depressed   A Pressing Concern A Starting Point Chapter 2) Gearing Up for Action   Here is our Plan Chapter 3) The Birth of Dep-Anon To Thine Own Self First Be True   A Great Lack of Understanding as to the Nature of Depression A Better Understanding of the Nature of Depression   Becoming Active Members of Dep-Anon Chapter 4) Being Part of the Conversation: A Collaborative Model Our Advocacy Role   Depression's effect on Families   Chapter 5) Dep-Anon Family Group: A Healthy Connection between the Depressed and the Family   Providing Leadership.

SECTION TWO

We're going to discover more details about how the mind of the depressed is dramatically impaired as they spiral further and further into that darkness of sadness. The feelings of helplessness and hopelessness dominate their lives. In Chapter Six, we begin to learn about the experience of depression and the gradual negative changes to the mind, body, and spirit of the one affected. We will reeducate ourselves on the best way to help the depressed. We learn that it is for us to understand the "why" they respond to the life changes as they do, sometimes with tragic results, sorry to say. We will discover that blaming them for their unwillingness to change (our mistaken assumption) is not helpful at all. With the proper assistance and support from their recovery program, the Depressed Anonymous fellowship, they can recover in their time frame and that with their commitment as an active member of their mutual aid group.

SECTION TWO: The Chapter headings and submenus are listed here in the order of their occurrence.

Chapter 6) What Is Depression A Sample of Negative Symptoms Creating Havoc In The Human Person A Sampling Of Some Of The Major Symptoms of Depression A Look Into The Mind Of The Depressed/Observations for The Family The Family Needs To Care for Itself. 7) Family Self-Care Where Do We Start? An Alternative Way The Turning Point Our Way Is Not Working/Family Takes A "Hands Off" Approach Most Depressed Are Not Aware Of The Cause of Their Lockdown. 8) Living the Solution We Are Not Alone 9) DEP-ANON is our North Star! We Felt Trapped. 10) Support of the Family is Essential. Our DSO Initially Has No Inkling of How To Turn Their Sadness Around. They Will Learn To "Fix" Themselves. Support of The Family Is Indispensable The Family Is Persistent In Taking Care Of Itself Family Support of Depressed Anonymous Meetings for Their DSO. 11) Do We Have A "Cure" Mentality? A Turning Point Limits and Boundaries Attending DEP-ANON Meetings regularly 12) The Importance of Belonging To A Mutual Aid Group We Are Never Alone!

First, the DEP-ANON is a necessary recovery program for the family and friends of the depressed. Here they learn about the crippling and life-threatening nature of depression. They will discover that their loved one or friend cannot just will themselves out of an incapacitating physical and mind-shattering problem. All the "snap out of it" and" get on with your life" messages directed at their depressed loved one are futile. Secondly, family members begin to see the necessity of taking care of themselves. With the DEP-ANON fellowship giving attention to Twelve Step living, it becomes clear that this is at the core of our personal and communal recovery.

"God grant me the Serenity to accept the things I cannot change. Courage to change the things I can, and wisdom to know the difference."

I thank the God of my understanding for helping all of us, family and friends, our depressed loved ones, all our programs of mutual support, united in hope, love, and service to each other according to their own needs.

"THERE IS HOPE ... AND WE DO RECOVER."

Hugh S.
Spring 2021
Louisville Kentucky

DEP-ANON PROVIDES HELP FOR FAMILY MEMBERS OF THE DEPRESSED

A PRESSING CONCERN

DEP-ANON promotes recovery for the family by learning more about depression as the family grows in acceptance and understanding. The depressed becomes aware of their life-threatening thoughts and behaviors that imprison and isolate them from family and friends.

By my decades-long involvement with the fellowship of Depressed Anonymous, I have stepped up my concern for the men and women suffering from depression. Now, I sense a pressing problem, a need to provide a recovery program modeled on the Twelve spiritual principles of Alcoholics Anonymous. Our emphasis is now on depression and not alcoholism. The family who deals with alcoholism in their loved one's life have AL-ANON. At this time in history, advocating for our Twelve Step Program of Recovery, we have DEP-ANON for family and friends of the depressed. In our newly formed DEP-ANON community, there is a place for family. Both can come and talk freely about their path out of helplessness and the debilitating feelings of being overwhelmed. In both groups, with time and work, they will discover how to use the recovery tools to live through the trauma with ongoing acceptance and understanding supplied by family and friends. Family members and the depressed find there is less hostility and hopelessness when their environments have improved, This will occur when there is more acceptance of the depressed significant other (DSO) on the part of the family of the depressed. The family is beginning to understand the nature and effects of the symptoms of depression. DEP-ANON family members will find their lives filled with peace, healing, and support with frequent sharing among themselves,

I find more effective and innovative approaches to the lessening of depression symptomology (syndrome) is the acceptance and support of the family, combined with the spiritual program of Depressed Anonymous.

The depressed person finds a supportive "surrogate family" in the fellowship of their mutual aid group. The family and friends of the depressed find equally valuable help in the friendship of their DEP-ANON group. Both of these Twelve Step groups produce a fellowship of acceptance and hope.

A conviction that what we offered for the depressed person, namely Depressed Anonymous, a program that will bring hope. The depressed have the tools to move step by step into a recovery program, feeling good about themselves and gaining self-confidence and hope. They found the tools and resources, but more importantly, they discovered persons like themselves. And now Depressed Anonymous groups are reaching around the world, all utilizing the spiritual principles of the Twelve Steps. We believe with the hope that DEP-ANON will have the same positive influence on the hurting families of the depressed.

(This next chapter is inserted here as a beginning examination of the Twelve Steps, with each new Step illustrating, with its theme, serving as a change agent for our own lives and the lives of those of our fellowship.

(Step One has as its theme that of acceptance. A few questions following each step can present topics for group discussion.)

STEP ONE: ACCEPTANCE
DEP-ANON FAMILY GROUP
DEPRESSED ANONYMOUS - STEP ONE
Reflections for individual and group meetings

STEP ONE: "We admitted that we were powerless over depression and that our lives had become unmanageable."

THEME: ACCEPTANCE

"How wonderful is the feeling that we do not have to be specially distinguished among our fellows to be happy. Not many of us can be leaders of prominence, nor do we wish to be.

Service gladly rendered, obligations squarely met, troubles well accepted, solved with God's help, the knowledge that at home or in the world outside we are partners in a common effort, the fact that in God's sight all human beings are important, the proof that love has freely given surely brings a full return, the certainty that we are no longer isolated and alone in self-constructed prisons, the surety that we need no longer to be square pegs in round holes and belong in God's scheme of things, these are the satisfactions of right living for which no pomp and circumstance, no

heap of material possessions, could be substituted."
(The Twelve and Twelve, p. 124.)

The primary reason that we come together as family and friends of the depressed is to help ourselves while supporting other family members like ourselves. We all desire to make a positive stand for our sanity and serenity. We have all tried to change, cure and cajole our beloved into health. By learning more about the nature of depression, we commit to taking care of ourselves, using the information gained to help ourselves. We all continue to suffer, feeling completely helpless and hopeless, struggling as a family to release our DSO from their prison of depression. We are learning that it is NOT up to us to heal and make our DSO healthy. It is our primary task to take care of ourselves.

By our fellowship with other family members, who also may share a life with the depressed, we admit that all we can do is take care of ourselves. We acknowledge that from this time forward, we are committing ourselves to the principle of "live and let live." We also espouse the four C's, which state our beliefs about NOT taking responsibility for the DSO's depression. These four C's can be a constant reminder of living each day with what we face.

The following are our four Statements of Belief:

1) I believe that I didn't cause it.
2) I believe I can't control it.
3) I believe I can't cure it.
4) I believe all I can do is to cope with it.

In Step One of our DEP-ANON fellowship, we admit that we are powerless over their depression. By taking responsibility for their every action, our lives gradually become swallowed up in the pain and sadness of the DSO's life. We gradually learn to let go of our impossible desire to fix and cure the depressed family member. We begin believing that what we CAN do is learn to cope with the depression and isolating behavior of our DSO.

We begin the healing journey with family members, discovering our path for healing and wholeness. It is precisely in the acceptance that we are powerless over our loved ones' symptoms of depression that our life of hope and serenity begins for ourselves. Neither can we make them happy. We can't make them think happy thoughts, which will send them skipping joyfully into life. We can't make them into us. We finally give up and accept the fact that we have no control over them - even though we stand on our heads day after day attempting to show them how much we love them. Again, this emphasizing that all we can do is try and cope with it.

We admit that we are powerless over them and their behavior. When we attempt to nudge our DSO into some positive activity, it goes unheeded. It turns out that our DSO is not angry with our daily exhortations alone, as we can learn later. They are genuinely immobilized and unable to move toward any positive and meaningful direction. It's no one's fault!

Family and friends look and see someone who looks healthy, with no outward signs that there is a physical problem, like a broken leg, arm, or other impairments. So, we think there is no good reason for them to continue lying around day after day with no future task that might motivate them into action.

The main idea of Step One is that we are at the point where we finally "get it" that our efforts to change our DSO will always fail. Our main thrust is to be supportive, non-judgmental, and uncritical. We are powerless over them and their behaviors. Our fellowship will now help us understand the nature of depression while giving us the critical and essential tools for taking care of ourselves. We begin to seek the support of other family members through the DEP-ANON fellowship and learn as much as we can about depression. We are not a medical group, nor are we a religious group. We do espouse a Higher Power who is at all times supporting our willingness, honesty, and openness to "let go" of our need to control the life of another human being. Step One creates that admission there is a God and isn't me.

Our DEP-ANON Family fellowship is NOT a therapy group, though its activities can provide a multitude of healing and hope. Another factor that helps us take care of ourselves is the collaborative nature of DEP-ANON. The mental health professional with a family physician and our DSO can come together to share their insights about the nature of depression.   Family members can learn positive ways to live their lives while serving as a significant resource for each other.

A STARTING POINT

A good starting point is for family members to learn the diagnosis of their DSO. In this way, they become partners in discovering the medications prescribed, including all side effects accompanying the various dosage of each medication. One prominent point here is that this collaborative is NOT a therapy group but serves primarily as an information and skill-sharing experience. Once the "red flags" of depression symptoms are identified, our DEP-ANON family members can discuss how they can be more effective and compassionate in their ongoing relationship with their DSO.

Psychologist James Hillman tells us, "until the soul gets what it wants, it must fall ill again."

For what does our soul yearn? Can you tell me? And How will this getting what the soul yearns make a difference in your mood and serenity?

"We can live now, and so we have to let go of our past hurts and resentments."

SAMPLE TOPICS/QUESTIONS FOR GROUP DISCUSSION

1) While living with your DSO, what is the hardest part for you to accept?

2) Have you tried to live more in the present, learning how to cope with the DSO?

3) Does belonging to a mutual aid group like DEP-ANON give you hope? Does it provide a solution-focused answer to living with someone depressed?

4) What types of efforts have you tried that have not worked for your DSO? Why not?

5) Can you accept the fact that your family feels powerless? What areas of your daily living seem unmanageable?

GEARING UP FOR ACTION

Hugh Smith founded the first Depressed Anonymous group in Evansville, Indiana, In 1985. There was little thought that this mutual aid group would expand beyond city limits. Years later, we have realized an important fact: depression is increasing worldwide as a global pandemic with tsunami force. It was clear that we needed a family group helping each other, learning ways to help themselves, and at the same time, while giving attention to their self-care, helping the DSO. Most of our family members never experienced the pain of depression, a life-threatening situation for many of our own and, for too many, ending in suicide.

We decided to create a fellowship, like Al-Anon, where family members are informed about the nature of depression. Because of the negative image that families sometimes have of their DSO's illness, they remain ignorant about what depression is and why it affects the whole family in the way that it does. We often hear a family member saying to the depressed, "Snap out of it!" as if to say that it is only a matter of having the willpower for them to get moving again. **That's the problem.** The DSO is powerless over the sadness that has immobilized their wills and incapacitated their bodies, a total debilitating experience. They are unaware of what they have until it's too late to stop.

Here is Our Plan

We have imitated Al-Anon's program to help members of the depressed family learn about depression and how it affects the mind, body, and soul and get the help we need. DEP-ANON deals with the nature of what depression is and what it is not. We work the Steps in our own lives and keep the focus on our attitudes and feelings, struggling to care for ourselves and our own physical and mental health. At the same time, we provide active support to those other members of the DEP-ANON fellowship. The critical and essential role for recovery is providing a sense of what depression is, learning more about it, resulting in a better position to give welcome support to our DSO – not more resentments and ill will.   And to keep the focus on ourselves. Our DSO will learn that it is up to them to take care of themselves. With this understanding, our lives will gradually become less stressful and filled with plans for putting more wellness activities into our personal lives.

The information shared at a DEP-ANON meeting provides emotional support through the personal stories and experiences shared by members of our fellowship. Our DEP-ANON group lives out multiple solutions in their own lives, gaining traction, restoring a feeling of control, putting the health and emotional well-being first, taking time and patience. We gain more sensitivity about how depression sometimes has its origins in early childhood. With time and their weekly sessions with other families and friends of the depressed, they discover ways to restore a healthy balance in our lives.

Families often feel stuck when a need arises to help their DSO. No matter what we do, nothing seems to help. An essential point for the DEP-ANON group is to help new members utilize the spiritual principles of the Twelve Steps. Our lives are based on those same principles that our DSO use for their recovery. These spiritual principles work for the fellowship of AL-Anon, and they are working for the DEP-ANON fellowship as well. You will begin to use the Steps as those tools designed to motivate your thinking and behavior to places you never thought would be possible.

(Step Two has Faith as its theme. Please examine the questions following Step Two and use the information as a possible topic for the group discussion.)

STEP TWO: FAITH
DEP-ANON FAMILY GROUP
DEPRESSED ANONYMOUS - STEP TWO

STEP TWO: Came to believe that a power greater than ourselves could restore us to sanity."

THEME: FAITH

Her daughter told Jane to get help. She saw the Depressed Anonymous group as the last chance for her mother, suicidal and despondent over the death of her husband a few months earlier. Jane didn't want to attend the meeting; she only came to please her daughter.

To tell a family member that they needed to get help has a familiar ring to those of us who have been physically exhausted as we tried to get our DSO up and moving in the morning but to no avail. Ultimatums hardly ever work where we are concerned. We have learned, the hard way, that trying to force our DSO into help, someone who doesn't want to change - continues to frustrate our efforts at helping. So, we have finally learned that the best source of helping others is first to get ourselves refurbished. Step Two is about being filled with faith in our self. This is especially true for those of us working on our DEP-ANON program of recovery

Now we have made a personal commitment to our healing by sharing in our support group, referencing our feelings of aloneness, inadequacies, and the direction our lives have taken. Anger so often keeps breaking through the surface of our lives. We are angry at our DSO. We are upset with ourselves for focusing our attention on the DSO instead of ourselves.   We soon find, ironically, that we mirror our DSO's feelings. We many times fill our minds with feelings of guilt and shame. The problem is that we still want to cure depression in our family. Our attitudes contribute to our continued failure to make the DSO feel better or to come out of their isolation and insane behaviors.

The Second Step is about faith. It is about taking our focus off our DSO and putting it where it belongs, on ourselves. The power which can free us from the pain of a fruitless effort to change another is the power of faith.

We are not alone because we now have a solution to feel relief from our isolation and helplessness, We are part of a family fellowship where we share hurts and feelings of frustration.

The great thing about being part of the DEP-ANON fellowship is that It reaffirms our faith that life is worth living. I no longer need to believe that there is nothing that I can do to feel better. But joined with me now are part of a vibrant fellowship and growing in a faith that they have not experienced before.

When I go to meetings, I continue to nurture tiny seeds of faith and hope that brought me into this community in the first place. I have discovered that the more I attend meetings and share my feelings, the more trust I have that I am on the right track.

I have always thought that if I could encourage more, pressure my DSO more, they would motivate themselves to initiate the change process. Wrong! Now I am beginning to learn that I must change if the world of my loved one is to change. Again, I know that the focus must be on my own need to change.

I am beginning to see that the more I study and apply the Steps to my situation, the less stress I create for myself. The group reminds me to review the four C's. With another reminder from the group to review the four C's. I am loosening my grip on the need to change others.

The more I believe in a power greater than myself, the more it begins to operate in my life. The more I let go of my perspective and turn it over to this greater power, I form a channel, a spiritual conduit. This power can enter into and slowly and methodically transform my life. With my life-changing, I find that those lives which I touch every day – they too begin to be changed. Now I know how life works - it is a paradox. DEP-ANON helps me focus my attention on what I need to do. The focus is no longer on the DSO but on where I am and how I will try and live one day at a time.

Whether my DSO goes to his Depressed Anonymous meetings or not – I have to take care of myself first. It is the only way I can maintain my sanity and learn from others the diverse and exciting ways God wants to lead us.

Bill W., the co-founder of Alcoholics Anonymous, tells us to believe more deeply. "Hold your face up to the light, even though for the moment you do not see." (As Bill Sees It, p. 7).

Thoughts from Bill W. can provide us with hope as we grow in our faith and commitment to be the best person we can be. We now have a plan which promises hope and wellness.

"It is by being part of the group that you will experience that miracle of the group, which is to find that a power greater than yourself is about to restore you to a feeling of serenity and personal hope." (Depressed Anonymous, p. 51).

SAMPLE TOPIC QUESTIONS
FOR DISCUSSION

1) How has being part of the DEP-ANON family group helped you find a power greater than yourself? How has this belief made a difference in your life? Please share with the group.

2) How difficult has it been to keep the focus on yourself? Do you still feel the DSO to be the target of your anger or resentments?

3) How have the four C's permitted you to free your mind from having to cure the DSO in your life?

4) Before DEP-ANON and your involvement in the group, what had been your notion of the Higher Power? Is having faith in a Higher Power helping to make your environment a more stress-free space? Share with the group.

THE BIRTH OF DEP-ANON
TO THY SELF BE TRUE

At the planning session for DEP-ANO, the family listed all their feelings living with their DSO. From the discussion, we were surprised to discover some amazing facts. First, we learned that the feelings family members were experiencing were very similar to their DSO's experience.

Secondly, these feelings were having an equally destructive effect in the lives of family members, as were the mood of their DSO.

When family members prioritized and described which feelings they experienced most often and most intensely, they produced the following list:

    1)   Feeling overwhelmed and burdened by a family member's depression

    2)   Feeling restricted around the depressed, feelings of something similar to the expression of "walking on eggshells."

    3)   Feelings of hopelessness

    4)   Anxiety about the situation and not knowing what to do about the feelings they were experiencing

    5)   Feeling emotionally drained

    6)   Feeling inadequate faced with a loved one's immobility and lack of motivation

    7)   Feeling anger and frustration at the DSO's behavior

    8)   Being an enabler and not liking it

9)   The DSO's life was unproductive, lacking motivation and, with a negative effect on family life.

10) Having feelings of irritability and impatience

11) Feelings of being inadequate

12) Unhappy

13)   Feeling betrayed by their spouse's late-life depression in retirement

14) Indecisive

15) Lack of confidence in oneself

A Great Lack of Understanding as to the Nature of Depression

One of the critical areas of concern voiced by the family was the lack of understanding of what depression is and how it affects the DSO. One of the members of DEP-ANON mentioned the night before the meeting, she and her daughter talked for hours, coming to a mutual understanding of what the daughter was experiencing. Was it that the mother was joining DEP-ANON and going for help that motivated her daughter to go for help? And her daughter came to the same conclusion: why did they both feel so bad living with a DSO and then to find out that their feelings happened to be the same as their DSO's?

It was then that the two women knew that this information that they shared could do a world of good for others like themselves. "We need a group like Al-Anon, where family members come together and learn how to keep the focus on their self-care." They want to move away from all their wasted energies and worry centered on their DSO, ignoring their concerns, always trying to take care of the family member

We came away from the first meeting of DEP-ANON with a good map of what the landscape would look like as we put together a support group for family members and friends of the depressed. And it was with these two women that DEP-ANON was born.

A Better Understanding of the Nature of Depression

For family members to understand depression, at least from the Twelve Step perspective of Depressed Anonymous need to read the introductory text of Depressed Anonymous. The founder of Depressed Anonymous wrote this book with members of the first mutual aid group of Depressed Anonymous. What could be better to understanding depression than to read the stories of the depressed and now living in recovery? They found the key that freed them from the dark and deadening isolation of the prison of depression.

One of the better ways for members of the DEP-ANON group to keep focused at their meetings is learning how to take care of themselves. It finally sinks in that family members have no control over the life and actions of the depressed. In other words, by admitting their powerlessness over their depressed family member, they realize that they have the same feelings as does their family member. Both family members, the family member who is a member of DEP-ANON, and their DSO begin their journey together, living out the Twelve Steps of recovery. The depressed significant other and the DEP-ANON family can now join others in their respective groups, persons like themselves, looking for and finding support, encouragement, and hope.

Becoming Active Members of DEP-ANON

Whether to attend Depressed Anonymous or not, the family commits themselves to be active participants in the fellowship of DEP-ANON. They hope their self-care program will focus on their own need. They will feel right at home with their new friends. They will learn how to focus on themselves, participate in the weekly meetings of DEP-ANON and get support and guidance as they use the tools suggested, enabling them to find answers to the questions that need answering. The mantra "To yourself first be true" continues to fill their minds. It's as if they have found the oasis in the middle of the desert. It is here that they start learning what depression is and what it is not. Now they know to use their recovery tools, the Twelve Step and, the Twelve Traditions. Their resolve Is focusing on themselves and not their DSO. Their weekly meetings provide them with ongoing energy to stay on the path of recovery. With participation in the DEP-ANON group, their mind focuses on their mental, emotional and spiritual health.

(Chapter Three has as its theme: Surrender and Trust. This theme can be a possible topic for discussion. Questions follow each of the Step commentaries.)

STEP THREE: SURRENDER AND TRUST
DEP-ANON FAMILY GROUP
DEPRESSED ANONYMOUS - STEP THREE

STEP THREE: "Made a decision to turn our wills and our lives over to the care of God as we understand God."

THEME: SURRENDER AND TRUST

"It is when we try to make our will conform with God's that we begin to use it rightly. To all of us, this was a most wonderful revelation. Our whole trouble has been the misuse of willpower. We had tried to bombard our problems with it instead of attempting to bring it into an agreement with God's intention for us. To make this increasingly possible is the purpose of AA's Twelve Steps. (As Bill Sees it, P. 43).

Now that we have charted a new course for ourselves in our relationship with our DSO, we will be open to every nudge and push that comes from our Higher Power. We will learn to listen to that small voice with quiet firmness telling us how to be of service to others around us. The voice that speaks to us on behalf of the other is the voice from the heart of God. We can discern the direction from where the voice comes, providing its guiding light for each of our lives.

Having a depressed loved one in our lives teaches us many things. We learn that no matter how hard we push, no matter how much we cajole them, all these well-intentioned efforts have not been able to produce any significant change in our DSO's moods.

I think we can agree that the only person we can change is ourselves. Please write this on your forehead.

An essential element in our renewal is the gradual loosening of our grip on the behavior of the DSO. We have learned a hard truth in "giving up" our control of what is to happen to our loved one or friend produce

The DEP-ANON fellowship would do themselves a world of good by attending a Depressed Anonymous meeting. It would allow us to enter into their loved one's world. Our DSO thrives, seeking help and healing support along with members of their recovery fellowship.

The time we spend taking care of ourselves can have an inverse effect on the condition and recovery of our DSO. The proof is the more we promote a positive emotional upbeat home environment, plus trying to understand depression, the more we will possess a new sense of identity as a survivor instead of a victim.

In the DEP-ANON family group, I can share my fears of our DSO crashing, their medications not working, and most seriously, are they having any suicidal ideations? All these fears push us down into the depths of personal doubt with fearful outcomes for our DSO. Sometimes our despairing moments are removed by living with hope. Our DEP-ANON program can provide many solutions for our DSO and ourselves. We continually turn our wills over to the care of the God of our understanding.

The continued isolation of our DSO puts enormous pressure on us to want to fix them, help them in every imaginable way. But by surrendering a need to make everything right for our beloved one, we begin to start work on ourselves. In the group, we all have been where other members have been – we have all reached the same path. We resented the fact that they were making our lives miserable. We were angry that they didn't get well fast enough to suit us. They were not on our schedule. They were unwilling to do it our way.

We now surrender our control – we make a decision here and now to "let go." We know that to increase our serenity, we must focus on the continued care of ourselves. Our experience makes it clear – the only way we are going to win is, in a way, a paradox. To win, we must lose our need to control. We continue to surrender our will, our control and hand it all over to God of our understanding. Our DSO must submit their fear of change to the God of their understanding. If they fail to do so, that's up to them, not you or me.

We are beginning a journey where our ticket to freedom is to trust other members of the DEP-ANON group with our unspoken fears, uncertainties, and anguish. We have found that if we are to get well ourselves, we will have to trust - someone from our fellowship whom we allow to enter our world of hurt and doubt. We remember that our focus has to be on ourselves. We want to move forward and find the hope that is promised to us when we allow our faith in God to provide us with trust for all our group family members. They now seem like old friends.

DEPRESSION QUESTIONS

1) Would you like to share your need to control my DSO? Have I made a plan to overcome this defect of character?
2) Has my perception of the God of my understanding changed since becoming a member of DEP-ANON?
3) Explain how I am becoming a part of the solution instead of being a part of the problem.
4) Is my trust in others growing now that I find a kinship with family and friends?

BEING PART OF THE CONVERSATION:
A COLLABORATIVE MODEL

Family members learn how to cope with their DSO by taking an active role in diagnosing and developing a treatment plan with those charged with their DSO's care. Because this is not just a relationship between a professional and their loved one but the whole family should be involved, contributing to the ongoing discussions centered on the DSO's wellbeing. The professionals need to invite, from the beginning, all those who want to be part of the DSO's treatment for recovery. The family cannot remain in the dark as to the progress of their loved one. The more the family knows, armed with a diagnosis, the better are they informed about the nature of their loved one's depression and the length of time needed for their recovery. With this information, instead of feeling outside the loop, the family is in a position to enhance their loved one's recovery.

Everyone can thrive with the complete collaboration from those charged with treating our DSO and the ongoing support from the DEP-ANON family group. They now have a legitimate role in the ongoing conversation affecting their DSO's life and future recovery.

Our Advocacy Role

Being an advocate for the depressed and the family's relationship with the medical and mental health professionals helps us become essential partners in all potential treatment modalities, now and in the future.

The family with their DSO can collaborate in their loved one's recovery. In some instances, a family can get the mistaken impression that they have no critical part or role in the ongoing care of their loved one. Possibly the family can feel even more unwanted, stressed, and sad.

Our DEP-ANON families, united together, serve as advocates for all in the community feeling helpless and alone. These folks are looking for someone or some others who provide a family the tools to lessen their frustrations while at the same time feeling more confident in being focused on their own lives instead of their family member who is depressed. Just as the DSO's found, we are finding being part of a DEP-ANON family group provides us with the strength to care for our needs. At the same time, we are learning to distance ourselves from that family member who is unable to respond to our love and help. We will join with those who have taken the plunge to work a spiritual program of the Twelve Steps and get a plan and become part of a spiritual recovery program that works for your benefit and causes you to flourish. We can no longer stay seated on the sidelines, wringing our hands, thinking that there is nothing that we can do to bring our DSO back to life. We feel that we have failed the one who needs us the most.

While we begin to learn skills to cope with a family member's depression, we also need the skills and recovery tools to deal with our own lives. Combined with those skills, we continue to cope and maintain our mental health and emotional balance. (See Appendix C for more on Recovery Tools).)

DEP-ANON is a better way to get the family to understand what depression is. As mentioned before, a family can feel isolated and disconnected from the health professionals - but only when they do not feel appreciated as essential partners in the care of their loved one. We continue with our efforts to learn more about depression, which will help alter our negative and judgmental thoughts about depression and the debilitating effect on the human person. The DEP-ANON family member will discover in time that unless the DSO has the positive support of the family, which extends from admission to the treatment center to the DSO's discharge, the hopelessness of the patient may end up in the same condition that got them there in the first place. We will watch how we speak to the DSO regarding their recovery and survival.

Depression's Effect on Families

We need to learn how depression can affect the whole family system. It's not just me and my DSO's symptoms of depression that need healing, but also our family and friends. We know that support groups are helpful for all those suffering from depression, including those of us who are participants in the DEP-ANON fellowship.

We are now engaged in looking inside ourselves, acknowledging that we didn't cause the depression and that we can neither cure nor control the depression. We do know that we can learn ways to cope. The depressed behavior appears to tell family and friends to "mind your own business" and for us to stay out of their lives. It looks that way, but I believe that in reality, the DSO's negative symptoms have made it difficult for them to get a clear picture of how their moods spiraling downward have distorted all feelings and attitudes toward their loved ones and closest friends.

A multitude of books having been written on the subject of depression. If you are like the rest of us, who have all run after the latest works on depression looking for answers, we believe that without doubt belonging to our DEP-ANON fellowship group will help restore balance and meaning in our lives. At the same time, our group's ultimate concern is finding solutions for the whole family, including our DSO's return, heralding a renewed emotional balance for all its members.

(The following chapter is a commentary on Step Five, whose particular theme is honesty. Questions following Step Four include questions as topics for the group discussion time.)

STEP FOUR: HONESTY
THE DEP-ANON FAMILY GROUP
DEPRESSED ANONYMOUS - STEP FOUR

STEP FOUR: "Made a searching and fearless moral inventory of ourselves."

Theme: HONESTY
"The perverse wish to hide one's motive underneath a good one permeates human affairs from top to bottom. This subtle and elusive kind of self-righteousness can underlie the smallest act of thought. Learning daily to spot, admit, and correct these flaws is the essence of character-building and good living."
(As Bill Sees It, p.17).

Indeed, our search of the soul - this mining of the soul will release the energy to proceed into the deep and dark recesses of our souls. The symptoms of our sadness and remorse force us to a search where we will shine the light of hope and trust – all the time being in the presence of a group of people just like ourselves. The DSO is also working through the Steps, and the family now finds that they can forgive themselves for not being perfect. We, too, can forgive ourselves for the anger that our family member arouses in us, many times to the point of exhaustion and exasperation. It's finally come to us to admit that we are not perfect, nor is anyone else. When we focus on our demons, we become aware that we have work to do. Now we are the ones who need changing. We have already admitted that we cannot change our DSO. We concluded that it is impossible to force change on a family member.

Understanding another takes time, patience, and a listening heart.

"There is a story about a circle that was missing a piece. The story centers on a circular shape-like creature missing a wedge-shaped piece of itself. It doesn't like this and sets out to find its missing piece, singing:

Oh, I'm lookin for my missin' piece,

I'm lookin' for my missin' piece,

Hi-dee-ho here I go,

Lookin' for my missin' piece.

It starts out on a grand adventure, searching for the perfect piece to complete itself while singing and enjoying the scenery. But after the circle finally finds the exact-sized wedge that fits it, it begins to realize that it can no longer do the things that it used to enjoy doing, like singing or rolling slowly enough to enjoy the company of a worm or a butterfly. It decides that it was happier when searching for the missing piece than actually having it. So, it gently puts the piece down and continues searching happily."

"The Missing Piece" by Shel Silverstein presents to us the lesson of the story that in some strange way, we are more whole when we are missing something."

As a family member, I must honestly face the ghosts in my own life and contend with how my inability to cure my beloved one forces me to look at my own life. I need to execute rigorous honesty as I take my own fearless and moral inventory of my strengths and deficits of character. In Depressed Anonymous, the depressed "believes that we will never have a respite from the pain of our loneliness and that the hell of our existence can only be relieved by numbing our sensitive feelings. We do this by withdrawing from others.

Just by expressing our feelings of loneliness and lack of support in our relationships with our DSO, who is depressed, we begin to feel the same isolation. I believe a lot of our difficulties have their roots in our need to be perfect and to do things the way others expect." (Depressed Anonymous, pg. 61).

Honesty is what I need for change to happen in my life, where we can now turn to ourselves and start the work that prepares us for a deeper application of the Steps for our lives.

Our DSO is used to our being there at all times and in every situation. We now know that this is impossible. The more we focus on ourselves, the more we will put more new wellness activities into our lives.

In Depressed Anonymous (p. 64), we believe   that "We are not here to condemn ourselves but to evaluate how we can achieve an inner peace promised to those who let go to trust in their Higher Power or the God of their understanding."

We can learn from each other in our mutual aid group of DEP-ANON about removing those defects of character that have kept us locked down in ourselves.

In our speaking with others in the fellowship about our feeling helpless and hopeless, rejected and alone, can in itself be the key that releases us from our depressed feelings and behavior. The depressed may be feeling they are living out their lives in a plan made by someone else.

One last reminder is "to thy own self be true." DEP-ANON is about learning how to take care of yourself. We have a plan and, we do recover.

SAMPLE TOPIC/QUESTIONS
FOR GROUP DISCUSSION

1) What steps am I taking to be true to myself today?

2) How can being honest with the DEP-ANON family group promise a healthier me now and for the future?

3) Is being part of the DEP-ANON group helping me be more honest about my character strengths and defects?   Give an example of how your behavior and thinking changed.

DEP-ANON FAMILY GROUP: A HEALTHY CONNECTION BETWEEN THE DEPRESSED AND THE FAMILY

"Each DEP-ANON Family group has but one primary purpose, to bring support to those family members and friends of the depressed. We do this by using the Twelve Steps and Traditions of DEP-ANON for our recovery informing, ourselves of the nature of depression and focusing on our physical, spiritual and, mental wellbeing. We cannot "fix" our depressed loved one." Tradition Five of the DEP-ANON Family Group.

DEP-ANON is a support group of family and friends of the depressed. This recovery program is much like Al-Anon, where family and friends gather to help each other learn how to detach from a DSO's resistance to change. The same approach applies to the families and friends to gather and learn how to live with their depressed loved one

With the publishing of Depressed Anonymous, the depressed have a book written by the founder of Depressed Anonymous with members of one of the first groups of Depressed Anonymous. This work continues to be a veritable fount of positive information, helping the depressed live out their lives in meaningful and purposeful ways. With the publication of DEP-ANON, those of us who have a depressed loved one as part of our family, we have our guide with suggested ways to live with serenity and an emotional balance.

Our DEP-ANON book, chapter by chapter, will lead families and friends into the many ways where we can build a strong relationship with our DSO, supporting us as we participate in our recovery. DEP-ANON is about taking care of ourselves, focusing on our recovery, and having the support of other families, all working together using the spiritual principles of the Twelve Steps. Every day our mantra, "To thy self be true," continues to motivate all our daily activities.

As members of DEP-ANON, we can begin to choose not to react to a family member, helping us refrain from criticism, anger, and frustration.

In Section Two of this work, we will discover more details about how the mind of the depressed is dramatically impaired as they spiral down further into the darkness of sadness. Here we learn about the experience of depression and the gradual negative changes that happen to the mind, body, and spiritual life of those affected. We know how to help the depressed understand why they respond in the way they do. We will discover that blaming them for their unwillingness to change is not helpful. They will change, but not in our time frame and not our immediate satisfaction. This will not help but will push them further into isolation.

We will understand that we didn't cause the depression. We learn that we cannot control. We find that we can't cure depression. We can try and live out our recovery program, focusing on our mental, spiritual, and emotional wellbeing. Our priority is to step back from our DSO, take a deep breath and realize that they will have to get the help they need while we continue to receive the support of our DEP-ANON family group.

As we are beginning to learn more about the nature of depression, we soon discover that there is no such thing as "snapping out" of depression. Similarly, this is like telling a person suffering from diarrhea to "snap out of diarrhea." It won't happen!

Providing Leadership

DEP-ANON provides leadership, helping us know how important it is to share our strength, hope, and experiences with all members at our group meetings. Our DSO has the opportunity to find help, either face to face or with an online group. Hopefully, in time, this can apply to the DEP-ANON fellowship.

We now know how we need to keep our emotions and thinking focused on taking care of ourselves. For us, this is particularly true as we learn how to detach ourselves from all the destructive worry and anxieties about our DSO. These anxieties keep us from focusing on ourselves and our recovery. We will find a roadmap that will gradually lead us out of our frustrations and into the light of hope.

DEP-ANON focuses on creating a relationship that creates an environment where the whole family, including our DSO, can find mutual healing. We will initially direct our DSO to Depressed Anonymous, where they can interact with others like themselves, utilizing the spiritual principles of the Twelve Steps and applying them to their own lives. We hope that what you read here will help you and help your DSO continue its recovery. We will always want to maintain our living the spiritual principles of the Twelve Steps, serving as our daily guide as we surround ourselves with our friends. These fellow travelers accompany each of us on our journey of hope.

(The Following Chapter Five has as its theme Courage. The theme can be used as a topic for group discussions. Questions follow each Step commentary.)

STEP FIVE: COURAGE
DEP-ANON FAMILY GROUP
DEPRESSED ANONYMOUS - STEP FIVE

STEP FIVE: "Admitted to God, ourselves, and to another human being the exact nature of our wrongs."

THEME: COURAGE.

We have learned that "Many times the desire to help the depressed may push the helper deeper into the isolation of the depressed - mirroring the reality of the depressed person." (Depressed Anonymous, Pg.186).

"One thing I've learned is that of all the horrendous problems we face in the world, what strikes me at the root cause of them all, and it's a myth, 'I don't have any power.'" Mark DuBois, Director of WorldWise.

"That which doesn't kill us will make us stronger." Friedrich Nietzsche.

Sometimes in our efforts to help the DSO, we often forget that our DEP-ANON recovery needs our attention. We need a fresh approach, and we need a plan. We can now admit that we became angry because our DSO didn't recover according to our schedule of events for their life. We might have even berated our DSO that all they had to do was pick themselves up by their bootstraps, and all would be well. We are beginning to learn new ways to take care of ourselves, and our eyes opened, and we find new strategies for helping ourselves.

We want to be conscious of the ways that have neither helped nor fixed our DSO's. Because our methods have not worked, this is no reason why we need to beat ourselves up over our past negative relationship with our DSO.

We might even begin to talk to our family about how we are learning how to keep our focus on our growth, taking care of ourselves.

We might tell them how we have found the support. We are now part of a Twelve Step group, DEP-ANON, which is for families and friends of the depressed. We are doing what we have asked them to do so we might have a better understanding of the nature of depression, and by doing so, we will have a better relationship with them.

"Our recovery begins the minute we turn our minds and our wills over to the care of God as we understood God." (Depressed Anonymous, Pg. 73).

It's beginning to dawn on us that just as the depressed need to do is get them back on track, the same applies to us. The same applies to ourselves.

We begin to admit that my own need to control my DSO has more to do with my own needs than those of the depressed. My need to "fix" mistakenly provided me with a sense of power and purpose for my own life. Families do care for their loved ones and, our DSO needs to take responsibility for their own lives and not be dependent on someone else.

We see that our emotional stability where we are no longer alone. Instead, we find ourselves in touch with a plan, actually 12 spiritual principles, joining with others like ourselves. Instead of casting any blame on the DSO, we now are in the active process of discovering those issues in our own lives that need work.

One of the issues that I will focus on is that of self-pity. I need to quit feeling sorry for myself. Trying to get my DSO back on track has been a failure. At first, we were encouraged how this or that new drug - the miracle pill - was supposed to do the trick. And when that didn't happen, we began to have a panicky feeling – we began to feel disappointed because it came back on us to make them happy again. Also, I felt angry when things didn't go well for my DSO. I wanted so bad for them to be the way they once were. The way they are now is hard to accept. At times, I am even angry at God for allowing all this sadness to be such a big part of our life situation. The sad events experienced by our DSO continue, completely rule my thinking, behavior and, moods.

I now know that our family fellowship, kindred spirits and all, will continue to give us a path providing us with hope and healing. The two references in the Steps are where we admit (Steps 1 and 3) that a needed change in our lives is necessary for everyone to grow.

SAMPLE TOPICS/QUESTIONS
FOR GROUP DISCUSSION

How has being an active member of DEP-ANON been a source of courage, helping me focus on myself and not on a family member or friend?

1) Where have I been able to find the courage to trust and believe that a Power greater than myself could restore me to sanity? Please give an example.

2) What am I learning about depression's effect upon the family? Please let us know, by example.

3) Are you surprised to discover that what you have been feeling with your DSO are some of the same feelings your loved one has been feeling? Please explain.

WHAT IS DEPRESSION?

The DEP-ANON fellowship learns that depression is a syndrome made up of various symptoms. Depression is not just feeling sad, but a system of multiple elements, resulting in our feelings spiraling downward, resulting in mild to moderate and, sometimes, a significant and potentially lethal depression.

Dr. Dorothy Rowe provides family and friends of the depressed with an excellent overview of what it feels like to be depressed. Every family member needs to read her Forward to Depressed Anonymous, Third Edition (2011). Her work will introduce you to some of the best writings today on the subject of depression.

"I believe that a more detailed description of the elements that make up the depression experience will help enlighten how depression is not a single thing, like a bacillus or a germ, but has many different parts forming what we call a syndrome. I think that just studying these various elements will help familiarize the family members with a great appreciation of what depression can do to a person's spirit and motivation abilities."

Depression is a closed system of symptoms.

All the symptoms in the closed system of depression are connected. When a change, either positive or negative, occurs, Dr. Rowe illustrates, with an example, how changes in two areas coinciding are more effective in treating depression than treating just one. This is why treatment may include medications, psychotherapy, and include peer-led support groups.

As noted previously, depression can spiral downward into a more profound mood. It furthers the saddening effect, sometimes leading from mild or moderate depression to major depression, including hopeless thinking, longer, more extended periods of isolation combined with suicidal ideation.

Depression is a closed system where elements of the plan directly influence another symptom in the entire system. This gradually causes an imbalance on the whole system – a domino effect, with time producing a spiraling downward of a deepening negative mood, eviscerating energy and motivation alike, placing the human person into lockdown.

A Sample of Negative Symptoms
Creating Havoc in the Human Person.

The following is a sample of how negative thinking and relentless ruminating produce a spiraling downward creating the negative moods deepening and intensifying hopelessness and helplessness.

This example is about a person who is already experiencing negative moods and negative thinking. This can cause a cascading effect so that the result is hopelessness, inactivity and, a lack of motivation. Let's look and read how this works out in the real world of a depressed person. An example of an inner dialogue might proceed in the following fashion.

"I feel too sad to do anything>>>>Besides, I'm ugly, sad, sick and tired and unable to do anything>>>>I don't feel like seeing anyone, so just leave me alone>>>>I don't have any enthusiasm for anything>>>>I'll just stay at home and sit around>>>>>I don't want to eat or sleep when it's time>>>>>I have no energy>>>>I'm really dull and uninteresting>>>>Maybe a drink or some pills will help me>>>> I shouldn't have done that, I feel awful this morning>>>> I've got to change>>>>But nothing seems to help>>>>I'm really a total failure>>>>I feel worse than before>>>>I feel really sad. What can I do? >>>>I feel too bad to do anything."

This example is typical of a depressed person who goes from one negative thought to another and ends up going in a circle, spiraling downward into that abyss called depression

A Sampling of Some of the Major Symptoms of Depression.

So, of the five major symptoms of depression - syndrome, one example of behavior – in the physiological symptom category, we see how an individual from no activity to getting in motion and walking. This is where a negative physiological symptom has turned into a positive change. As before, our DSO was tired all the time, imprisoned in one of the symptoms of the closed system, that is., no physical activity. He now discovers that his changed thinking has changed his feelings. After walking, he believes he will feel better if he keeps up his walking activity, there is a positive change in time. "Motivation follows action!"

When his thinking went from feeling hopeless to feeling hopeful, here was another positive that helped him break out of the closed system that had him imprisoned and enslaved. Even though his future looked bleak, he was able to take the plunge and get himself motivated to move the body with his mind close behind. He now could see the light at the end of the tunnel. The longer he believed his walking could be the start of getting better, the more he continued to walk. (A fact experienced by the author). His positive belief (his thinking) plus walking (his physical activity) created the ability to get out of the symptoms that kept him imprisoned. But likewise, his deepening mood (feelings) began to lighten as he believes that changing one's behavior does produce positive results.

It is encouraging to know that by changing one or two negative symptoms in the closed system of depression, discover that we can make a significant crack in our prison wall, gradually setting ourselves free. We are all encouraged by this fact.

The depressed learns how to break out of the prison of depression, with its' life stifling closed system of depression. For the depressed, this goal is made possible by being part of the Depressed Anonymous fellowship. And this getting moving also works its' wonder for those of us in the family group.

A Look into the mind of the Depressed

To paraphrase Bishop Vallejo's statement, he shares with us that "When a family member is depressed, the family suffers and feels disoriented - the family system is off balance. Conflicts and anger start to flare up. On the other hand, the family is the best therapist for a depressed person. However, it is not unusual for the family believes that the depressed family member is a hypochondriac. The support of the family is indispensable. But this is where we encounter the great problem - the best help for the treatment of the DSO is for the family to take care of themselves." The Archbishop of Seville, Spain, Carlos Amigo Vallejo, **The**

Spiritual and Pastoral Care of the Depressed Person and Family, pp .142-146. In Dolentium Hominen, No. 55 – Year xix -No-1, 2004 Journal of the Pontifical Council for Health Pastoral Care, Vatican City, Italy.

Observations for the Family

"We are face to face with a person who has fallen into indifference, who is personally tired – his life has become an uphill struggle and freeing himself of it would be a great liberation: a person who spreads pessimism and tiredness, thinks that he is useless and cannot be rehabilitated, is interested in nothing, and walks through the world with anxious hope and an enormous feeling of guilt.

But for this person is not a mere patient with specific pathological symptoms – he is family. For the depressed, it is improbable and practically impossible to make any decisions. They suffer, but they do not know what is happening to them: they make others suffer, and everybody feels dismayed and undefended and abandoned." Archbishop Jorge Enrique Jumenez Carvajal. **The Role of the Family Faced with Depression**, pp. 140- 141. In Dolentium Hominum, 2004.

I have felt this way many times, totally without the ability to change the other, the DSO. I found the best way to help is NOT to help. Sound uncaring? A paradox? Yes, it does sound that way, and we know family members feel the same way. They feel as helpless as the depressed. Many of us have tried everything to help our DSO but to no avail. It seems that what we say or do pushes them further away from our help and, this is even more so when we are critical and show hostility toward them.

The Family Needs to Care for Itself

Al-Anon promotes the argument that the family needs to take care of itself and does so by learning as much as is possible about the disease of alcoholism. They discover how alcoholism affects the whole family system. Our recommendation for family members of the depressed is to learn as much about depression as possible. DEP-ANON operates out of the same belief: Take care of yourself by being part of a group program of recovery specifically centered on depression and how it affects the whole family.

(Chapter Six has as its theme, Courage. This theme can be a potential topic for group discussion. Questions follow each of the individual Step commentaries.)

STEP SIX: COURAGE.
DEP-ANON FAMILY GROUP
DEPRESSED ANONYMOUS - STEP SIX

STEP SIX: "Were entirely ready to have God remove all these defects of character."

THEME: COURAGE

"Self-pity is one of the most unhappy and consuming defects that we know. It is a bar for all spiritual progress and can cut off all effective communication with fellows because of its inordinate demands for attention and sympathy. It is a maudlin form of martyrdom, which we can ill afford." (As Bill Sees It, Page 238).

In "A Victim in my Mind," a member of the Depressed Anonymous fellowship shares her personal story where she often saw herself as a victim of life's circumstances.

"I had always been hard on myself. I reamed myself every time something bad had happened. 'Why can't I find someone to love me?' 'Why isn't God looking after me?' But for some reason, when I realized that I was doing this to myself, it made me realize that maybe all I have to do is stop doing it. So, if I tell myself positive thoughts, eventually I'll have to feel positive." (Depressed Anonymous, P. 120).

To change one's life, one must be willing to make some personally drastic changes in how we think, feel and act.

Thinking about what must be changed today, when we think about what needs to be changed in our lives, we must tackle the task of learning more about what depression is all about. We are concerned that our loved one is willing to do all in their power to take care of themselves, by going to DA, taking their medications as prescribed, going to therapy, or all of the above. In a previous chapter, a family has a part in the conversation with health professionals about the mental and physical health of their DSO. We know now that we must be in the loop about suggested treatment plans for our DSO.

"We learn to change not the world, but how we view the world and all its intricacies." "The Higher Power whom I choose to call God is there to help me at any time I ask. And you know what? He rescues me every single time?" (Depressed Anonymous, P. 134).

Also, "Depressed Anonymous finds that just a willingness to believe is enough to start a personal program of recovery. The desire to flee from the pain of my sadness becomes greater than the sadness which depression holds over me." (Depressed Anonymous, P. 78).

So often, the DSO, with their resistant behavior toward all our pleadings, makes us feel restricted in the way we lead our lives. We realize that the more we keep our attention and energies fixed on the intransigence of the other, the less time for the needed work on our damaged emotions. Our healing takes shape when we sharpen our focus. Progress, not perfection, is our daily mantra.

Since I have decided to change, I want to refrain from worrying about my DSO's situation. That decision in itself motivates and inspires me to ramp up efforts at taking care of my own needs.

Just as the depressed isolates and distances from everything and everybody (a symptom of their sadness), their emotional wellness can begin when they begin making an effort to connect with others like themselves. These people are to found at the regular meetings of Depressed Anonymous. So too, all of us in DEP-ANON know that there is strength in being with other families who like, us, have a depressed loved one as part of their family.

Now that we are willing to get involved in our recovery - more recovery will be ours. The less involved we are with the DSO, the more responsibility they can take for their recovery. Remember, we cannot cure or take responsibility for anyone's depression – we can only be responsible for ourselves. We can cope as we can and continue to utilize our DEP-ANON recovery program.

The fellowship and friendship which I find in DEP-ANON motivate me to be more active in the care of myself.

We have emphasized willingness as being indispensable. Are we ready to let God remove from us all the things we have admitted are objectionable? Can God take them all? If we still cling to other people, such as our DSO, and we begin to pray that we might let go. We ask God to help us be willing. It's a good start. When ready, we say something like this "My creator; I am now willing that you should have all of me, good and bad. I pray that you remove from me every single defect of character which stands in the way of my usefulness to you and my fellows. Grant me strength as I go on from here to do your bidding." (Depressed Anonymous, P. 82).

SAMPLE TOPICS/QUESTIONS
FOR GROUP DISCUSSIONS

1) In my willingness to let go of my character defects, as I have listed in my 4th Step inventory, I am finding a new sense of purpose unfolding in my life. Please explain.

2) Show how you are willing to let God control your life. How has this belief provided you with a better relationship for you and your depressed friend or family member?

3) Now that I have been more willing to give our DSO their space, how has this helped us? Has learning more about the nature of depression helped in this regard? Explain how this has helped in your own life and the lives of family members.

FAMILY SELF-CARE. WHERE DO WE START?

Learning all that we can about the nature of depression is one of the principal ways to understand what depression is or is not. Now we can reflect upon the four C's and discover their common-sense approach for those wanting to help themselves. We want to focus on those skills and information for those family members who look for a plan and execute it. It's about self-care. Similarly, it's about the futility of blaming oneself for the condition of a loved one or friend who is depressed. We start with the four C's.
It may even be helpful to say them out loud.

I didn't cause it
I can't cure it
I can't control it
I can only cope with it.

Family members soon learn that willpower is no use in the DSO's leaving their prison of depression. There is no good in family members expressing hostility, anger or feeling guilty about their relationship with their depressed loved one. Some call this negative behavior "expressed   emotion." Instead of helping, the family's negative attitude continues to drive a wedge between family members and their DSO. It gives the depressed family member a reason to isolate and to continue building a higher wall of isolation,

THE PAIN OF THE DEPRESSED IS REAL!
PLEASE, NO "SNAP OUT OF IT" COMMENTS.

When we, the family, understand the nature of depression, it's feasible that the acceptance of the loved one may gradually bring about this attitude change in ourselves. It is the understanding of how the pain of the depressed is real. The family only does more harm when it says things like "snap out of it" or "just go out and get a job" or "join the human race." But for one depressed, their body, filled with fatigue and lacking motivation for every thought, every task, every decision, becomes a Herculean effort., The depressed individual, to use a metaphor, is stuck in neutral. Because we have not experienced depression ourselves, we are limited to understand fully. We see what appears to be a healthy-looking individual complaining that they can't get out of bed, can't look for a job, can't make a doctor's appointment, can't, and don't want to. How can that be, we ask ourselves? The talk in the family is that he or she is "just plain lazy."

An Alternative Way

We are finding an alternative way to help our depression. The best way now is to learn how to take care of ourselves and leave the results up to God or our Higher Power. We admit to having no control over our DSO, tend to want to abandon our DSO, thinking that with the recovery tools, we still were not able to move our beloved out of their depression and isolation.

Ironically these same tools of recovery can be used both by the DSO and the family. These tools promote a healthy plan for taking care of ourselves. (Information about the recovery tools can be found in Appendix C).

Now we relax, take a deep breath and begin our work. DEP-ANON has provided the Twelve Steps as the ladder, helping us climb out of our hole while our support group continues to help us understand depression and how it dramatically affects our DSO. It is here, as families, that we can admit our helplessness, unmanageableness in dealing with our family members. In the discussion time or testimonies at our DEP-ANON meetings, we begin to feel the pressure subsiding as we begin to learn the "how" of taking the focus off our DSO and putting it on our feelings of helplessness. By creating some distance between the DSO's needs and our own, we have to give up control. With work, prayer, and group support, we finally realize that it is not up to us to "fix" our DSO. We soon learn how to quit our "white-knuckling" as we see our DSO ignoring our advice on how to go about using a ready-made recovery program, no matter how hopeless they are feeling.

Our Way is not Working

And now as, a member of DEP-ANON, we realize that our way of criticizing and complaining does not make any changes in our DSO's thinking, feeling and behaviors. The more we persist in trying to "fix" him or her, the more we push them away. All our efforts are effectively fruitless. So, we withdraw from them and their "obstinacy" toward our wanting to "fix." We have hit a brick wall. Now we are ready to seek help from the spiritual principles of the Twelve Steps of recovery and live them out each day in our lives and with relationships.

Family Takes a "Hands Off" Approach

We begin to see the light. Our DSO discovers that we are taking a "hands-off" attitude toward them. Armed with our knowledge of the nature of depression and the torment and potential risk to the lives of those who suffer from depression, we realize that they are not to blame for depression. They are mentally, physically, and emotionally unable to turn on and off, like a water faucet those negative feelings and thoughts which have beat them down into submission. Their deepening sadness has left them unmotivated, immobilized, believing there is no way out. At the starting point in our recovery, dealing with the frustration and anger experienced in the family, we decided too completely back off. With our involvement in the group, we find the solution to our frustration. The answer is to begin to focus on ourselves. We will take care of ourselves as a family and as friends. We are all together in this effort to regain our sense of commitment to ourselves. We know that taking care of ourselves is the right thing to do.

(Chapter Seven has as its theme HUMILITY. This theme can serve as a potential topic for group discussion. Questions follow each of the individual Step commentaries.)

STEP SEVEN: HUMILITY
DEP-ANON FAMILY GROUP
DEPRESSED ANONYMOUS - STEP SEVEN

STEP SEVEN: "Humbly asked God to remove our shortcomings."

THEME: HUMILITY

In Steps Four and Five, we wrote down and shared our list with another person the exact nature of our wrongs. Now in this Step, we are asking God to remove our shortcomings. God only knows that we have them. And just as it does no good to continually criticize the DSO, continuing to beat up on ourselves is likewise fruitless.

If humility means truth, then we need to find out how truth w set us free as we mine the soul for all those defects of character keeping us from looking at "the plank in our eye." Even though we are antagonistic toward our DSO because of the lack of knowledge of what depression is, we still serve ourselves well to take a deeper look into our own lives.

Willingness is the starting point whether or not we want to proceed further with our recovery. For now, we want to share with our group that we are willing and ready to do all in our power to keep the focus on what we need, leaving the rest for God to continue working in our life.

In As Bill Sees It, pg. 10, Bill tells us that "Self-searching is the means by which we bring new vision, action, and grace to do all in our power to bear upon the dark and negative side of our nature." With it comes the development of humility makes it possible for us to receive God's help. Yes, it is only a Step. We will want to go further.

We will want the good in us all, even in the worst of us, to flower and grow. But first of all, we shall wish for sunlight, as nothing much can grow in the dark. Meditation is our out in the sun."

To ask God to remove our shortcomings when we never thought we had any – at least any that amounted to anything. Now that we are active in the fellowship, we know how it was difficult at first to let God remove anything. We found that thought a bit too intimidating. We were worried that we might end up being the hole in the doughnut. But the more God or the Higher Power revealed itself to us in the group fellowship, and we saw how it eventually made us more trusting and more assured of God working things out for us in our own lives. If God could do it for others, he surely would do it for us as well. This humility also helped us become accepting and more apt at understanding the life and struggles of the DSO and those friends with whom we share our lives. Much of the understanding has come about by our newly won insights into the nature and complexities of the experience we call depression.

Put this on your forehead: There is a God - it ain't me."

Most Depressed are not Aware of the Cause of their Lockdown

Reading a book about depression or experiencing depression where others share personal struggles helps us understand how this is a deadly and severe problem confronting our loved ones. We also know that we cannot change our loved ones - even though we have tried to do all we can to make them feel better. Humility comes as we finally accept the truth of the situation, and we know that they have to want to change before they can change. We are beginning to understand how difficult it is to change or what even to call what paralyzes their will and motivation. Like most of us, depressed or not, facing the uncertainty of life is not something we cherish.   For some depressed, the fearful thought pops up in their mind "why change and possibly get something worse than what they have now?

To accept the fact that we require a change ourselves is another critical point of recovery. We are beginning to believe that when I surrender and trust my Higher Power and my group that life starts for me.

SAMPLE TOPICS/QUESTIONS
FOR GROUP DISCUSSION

1) What shortcomings has God removed from our lives that we care to share with the group?

2) Truth is humility, and humility is truth. Please share how the group has allowed you to find the truth(s) about yourself?

3) Is it possible that our attitude toward our DSO might be one of the reasons for our DSO to retreat from our family and us? What are some of your thoughts which might explain our DSO moving away from us into further isolation? (See Appendix A)

LIVING IN THE SOLUTION

When we examine our own lives, we discover, like our DSO, that we need a plan that works. We already have experienced the power of the Twelve Steps. We know they can work. In this respect, both the DSO and the DEP-ANON family group have come to believe that a power greater than ourselves will restore us to sanity.

Now let's get on with our self-care and begin that adventure and journey with others like ourselves. DEP-ANON can be a powerful experience strengthening each of us as we continue to help other family members, as we provide help to each other. We are discovering how the best care for others is to care for ourselves. We are learning that we must live in the solution, focus on it, and practice the skills solidifying our efforts to maintain mental wellness and a balance in our lives.

Initially, the depressed and family members can help find the doctor, find the necessary medication, the therapist, and the Depressed Anonymous support group. The DSO will have a plan and a healthy combination of therapies, which will help put them into contact with the mental health and medical personnel for their ongoing care, now, and into the future. After that, we may leave worry behind, take our focus off of our DSO's recovery progress and move into our recovery. We remind ourselves to maintain the essential four C's in our lives. Hands off! We all continue learning that the depressed and family members have pretty much the same problem - all suffering directly or indirectly from the ravages of depression.

Family members and friends of the depressed discover that we may feel helpless and restricted as the depressed. (See Chapter Three) But one thing that we have going for us is the same thing that the depressed have going for them. **We have choices.** We know that their involvement in their group and speaking up at support group meetings will gradually restore sanity to their thinking, feelings, and behavior. Their involvement can provide them the support needed to work through their problems. To help them with their progress, they will have a sponsor. Since our recovery program is the same, based on the Twelve Steps, the pain in the life of the depressed family member is at some level the same as our own.

We are Not Alone

We know now that we are not alone. We are in this effort together with other family members. We are coming together – not to complain and blame the depressed about their problems. We all come together to live in the solution of a program based on spiritual principles, just like the depressed who can get needed help and support from their mutual aid group, Depressed Anonymous. No attempt will be made by us to try and fix our DSO – we know that is impossible. One of the more positive things for a family member to know is that their loved one cannot simply "snap out of" depression. It is impossible! We discover that no matter how often and intently other ill-informed persons encourage them to do so, it is still humanly impossible. Depression is such a powerfully painful experience that only those who have lived within its high walls of isolation can know the pain.

One of the first efforts in overcoming one's need to fix and care for one's loved one's depression is learning how to let go and let the Higher Power work out its plan in the life of the DSO. We wouldn't want to get ahead of God, would we?

(Chapter Eight has as its theme Forgiveness. This theme can be a potential topic in our group meeting discussions. Questions follow each of the individual Step commentaries.)

STEP EIGHT: FORGIVENESS
DEP-ANON FAMILY GROUP
DEPRESSED ANONYMOUS – STEP EIGHT

Step Eight: "Made a list of all persons we had harmed and became willing to make amends to them all."

THEME: FORGIVENESS

"To be living with a person depressed is to experience their lows and feel as trapped as they do. If you have been sad and depressed over any length of time, just know that it has adversely affected people around you."

Forgiveness is the idea that summarizes this step for those of us who are members of the DEP-ANON family group. To forgive is making a move to let go. To forgive is to say, "I am sorry." To forgive means that I no longer intend to criticize the person that is depressed. We now know that no matter how depressed our DSO or friend might be, our criticism will make matters worse. We need to remember that we are learning about the nature of depression and how it can completely immobilize a person. We might even make amends to the family members and tell them that we are getting help (DEP-ANON) and, we are going to learn more about depression. As a member, we need to forgive ourselves and how we have dealt with our DSO. Our way was not helping anyone get well; instead, it was just pushing us apart. We became angry at the depressed and ourselves. Thanks to the Step program of recovery and our fellowship, we are beginning to forgive ourselves for not being perfect. We have to continue with our DEP-ANON program and stay focused on our recovery. We admit in Step One how we have been operating out of ignorance of what the nature of depression is.

To forgive anyone is to break the chains that bind us. We need to forgive parents, institutions, and those we feel we have hurt because of our lack of understanding of depression. For some, it may even lead to suicidal ideation and completed suicide.

Just like the depressed, we learn that to be free, we have to free ourselves from resentments and those deep negative feelings causing our relationship with our DSO to get worse instead of better. We all know how compulsive behaviors can affect the lives of others. In this Step Eight, a powerful statement how our family member's depression, with its various symptoms, can have a detrimental effect upon the family.   Remember depression, can be contagious.

"In my field of counseling," states the author of Depressed Anonymous, I have always tried to help the family of the depressed. I have wanted to make the whole family a part of the conversation. The entire family needs to be involved in the healing process. DEP-ANON, people like ourselves have at their disposal those materials that can enable us to take advantage of how to care for our own lives before we try to change others.

As you progress in understanding, you see that other family members, like you, are relieved to get new insights into communicating with the hurting, depressed family member. This progress is huge for restoring a healthy balance in the lives of all family members.

Many family members shared how it was possible for them to feel so much anger and frustration with a family member who was sick? Good question.

Most of us have little understanding of the depression experience. The most positive response to this question is to learn more about some of the causes that may have brought your DSO to the point where they are today.

So, forgiving the other may be a more significant large issue in our recovery journey. To forgive is to clean off the slate of hurts, anger and, resentments. What appeared to be an easy process for the DSO to change turned out to be a learning challenge, not an impossible challenge for family members. This program causes us to commit ourselves, just like our family DSO who needs to be embedded in a mutual aid group and committed to recovery.

SAMPLE TOPICS/QUESTIONS
FOR GROUP DISCUSSIONS

1) What would be your response to the family member who claims how difficult, if not impossible, to forgive all the pain that the DSO has put them through? In actuality, what was the process of healing that got you to the point of forgiveness?

2) What lessons have the group members of DEP-ANON given you to forgive? Please share your response.

3) Have I begun to understand the complexities that make up the illness of depression? Is it your belief that depression is experienced in the same way for everyone? (Depressed Anonymous, P. 95).

DEP-ANON IS OUR NORTH STAR!

Since our program is spiritual, we make no apologies to anyone for our need to place our trust in this power greater than ourselves. We admit that since we cannot make our depressed loved one feel better - we discover with gratitude that we are no longer alone in this effort. We now have a supportive family group, providing ways to care for ourselves. We believe that good things are bound to happen now that we are no longer struggling alone and are part of a proactive fellowship that provides its members with the needed positive resources for change.

Right now, I am going to leave my loved one for a spell. No longer will my DSO find a residence in my mind, occupying my every thought, keeping me fixated on their every negative mood. We have been riding the waves of torment and hopelessness for months and even for years without a break. We felt that we had no place to go. This mental negativity always promoted a downward spiral in our moods and behavior. Can I say that we were stressed! Because of the stress, we sometimes found ourselves hospitalized. We thought our heads might pop off with our pent-up emotions. Without DEP-ANON, we felt like a ship without a rudder to keep our courage up. We found ourselves alone and without any support as we tried to get us through the days and nights of our failure to bring our loved one back into the family circle

We Felt Trapped

An obvious fact we have learned is that our DSO's are not as different from us as we would like to think. When it comes to us, we recognized and admitted to ourselves and others that we were shackled with the same darkness as was our DSO. We felt trapped. And what did we do about it? Nothing. We had hit a wall. Amazingly, it is like looking into a mirror, and instead of seeing ourselves, we see our DSO. Do we feel we have lost our very selves in all of the chaos that has been an ongoing, daily part of our lives?

The lesson that family members need to reflect upon, with feedback from the DEP-ANON fellowship, are all the myriad aspects of depression that we discussed in Chapters Six and Seven. Some say that it is like being in an eighty-foot hole with only an 8-foot ladder. Others say that it is like being in a dark room with no windows, no door, and having no way out! But we at DEP-ANON have each other, with a program that works. And we are gradually laying out a path in our life based on the dynamic spiritual principles of the Twelve Steps.

Many times, we hope that our depressed family members will continue with their recovery program practicing these principles of the Twelve Steps every day.

(Chapter Nine has as its theme Freedom. The theme can is a potential topic for group discussion. Questions follow each of the individual Step commentaries.

STEP NINE: FREEDOM
DEP-ANON FAMILY GROUP
DEPRESSED ANONYMOUS - STEP NINE

STEP NINE: "Made direct amends to another except when to do so would injure them or others."

THEME: FREEDOM

Again, we strive to clear up the wrongs and shortcomings in our lives. At times, we needed to make amends to our loved ones for our impatience and lack of compassion and consideration for the pain that filled their lives.

We know life sometimes includes a need to admit our wrongs to another. We need to make amends. We have already made a fearless and moral inventory of our lives and amends, need to be made.

Learning more about the Twelve Steps furthers growth and, our strengthened motivation will be to continue ways to take care of ourselves, focus on ourselves by doing so, find that our loved one's life isn't managed and controlled.

Maybe we weren't conscious of a need to being more aware of how we reacted to our DSO. We felt that we knew what the problem was, so there was no real need to look inside ourselves, putting a **spotlight** on our behaviors. We didn't have a problem – our family member has the problem.

Having a member in our family who suffers from depression is often cause for talk and concern among our family. Sometimes there is more negative judgment than care, more criticism than concern, more hostility than compassion. As family members and friends, we are beginning to learn how there will be other options that we will pursue our spiritual and emotional health.

Freedom is what we are about here. We want to dig out, find the time and the courage to understand our grievances, discovering how best we can help them, and take care of ourselves too. Serenity is the rightful outcome of making peace between ourselves and those we are making amends.

Now that we have taken Steps in restoring any broken relationships, we now move ahead and place ourselves in a recovery program with others, fitting us well and living life one day at a time.

One of the better ways to make amends is to commit yourself find peace and serenity. We each begin to take responsibility and control over our lives and quit blaming other people in our family, ourselves, institutions, or our jobs for the sadness that we feel, and move on under the umbrella of forgiveness and compassion.

If we make a mess, we clean it up. Now! We will no longer ruminate about our DSO and the pain they have been causing our family by not taking responsibility for themselves. We soon will learn or have learned that our loved one is physically, mentally, spiritually and, emotionally incapable of springing to their feet, gleefully telling the family that everything is OK now. Recovery can take months and even years for our DSO to respond consistently to applying the Twelve Steps to their lives.

We will let our depressed family member find their way as we continue to choose the DEP-ANON recovery tools for recovery.

SAMPLE TOPICS/QUESTIONS
FOR GROUP DISCUSSION

1) Do I suffer guilt about my negative past relationship with my DSO?

2) How does it feel to make amends to my DSO? How do I intend to use my new awareness of the disabling power of depression for the repairing of familial wounds?   Please explain. (Depressed Anonymous, Pgs. 102-103).

3) With a new understanding of the nature of depression with its' negative effect upon the human person, how has this increased my freedom to see my DSO and myself in a new and positive light? Please explain this change to the group.

SUPPORT OF THE FAMILY IS ESSENTIAL

"However, it is not easy for a depressed person to express their feelings. He has lost all willpower. In extreme cases, he may have even lost the will to speak. At the base of a depressive state, there seems to be an indefinite and oppressive fear of living, a fear of life. It is said that as long as there is life, there is hope. In this case, both things are absent. The quality of life is very low and, hope has disappeared. With one's quality of life diminished and, pain can be like a wall that separates us from God, family, and friends. It is not surprising that the depressed may blame God for the state in which they find themselves. "

Cardinal Carlos Amigo Vallejo, **The Spiritual and Pastoral Care of the Depressed Person and His Family**, p.142. Dolentium Hominum (Depression) Vatican City, 2004.

Depression, as we know, enslaves, detaching the DSO from self, the world of family, and good friends. Their life is held captive in prison with the invisible bars. They are in lockdown. The depressed perform their most basic human needs with resistance.

The DSO of our families has lost a sense of their own identity, no longer feeling competent to do all that they had previously enjoyed doing. This loss of competency prevents them from engaging in those occupations once provided them with a sense of achievement and purpose. In itself, this loss of a life with meaning and direction is severe.

And as necessary as the reality of being connected with human relationships, they have cut off all relationships, including family and friends. No one is accompanying them, either as a friend or loved one. The individual has also lost their autonomy to make decisions, a personal power reflecting a sense of staying productive and goal-centered. They are on the periphery of life. They no longer can thrive.

"Accompanying and family solidarity are always advisable in helping those who are at the doors of depression or who are already in its clutches.

It is better to be accompanied in a process that may well be slow but which includes a plan of practicable and concrete activities that include physical, intellectual, recreational, religious and, social activity."

H.E. Msgr. Jorge Enrique Jiminez Carvajal, Bishop of Zipaquira, Columbia. Member of the Pontifical Council For Health Pastoral Care. The Role of the Family Faced with Depression, p.141. Dolentium Hominum (Depression), 2004, Vatican City.

Our DSO initially has no idea of how to turn their sadness around They will learn to "fix" themselves.

We know a person whose negativity and gloom are similar to contracting a contagious virus, infecting those around them. People feel like they are walking on eggshells when they are around their DSO.   The depressed have lost all interest in living and, they also feel personally unacceptable to themselves and others.

Their ability to make decisions are fruitless. Guilt, shame, and anxiety continually fill their minds and thinking. The depressed wants to figure out what is happening to them and questions why. They have lost all hope. And because they have no understanding of the nature of depression or even the major symptoms of depression, they have no understanding of how to turn their desperate situation around. The depressed wonders what is wrong with them: no answers are forthcoming.

As mentioned, so many times before - trying to help the depressed does not make the sadness disappear. Family members "expressed emotions," meaning their hostility and criticism, make matters worse.

Hopefully, with a DEP-ANON fellowship with that refreshing openness to what depression is and how it affects their DSO, a new spirit can exist in the family circle and giving life to a new family environment. We have already examined in some detail, in Chapter Six, the causes of depression, yet, the DSO was not aware of the recovery tools, and if used, could have helped prevent the spiraling down of our DSO's thinking and wellbeing.

Now, I can say for me personally that I am aware of the "red flags" alerting me to a possible downward spiral if attention is not given to the use of those recovery tools. I make daily use of my recovery tools. (See Appendix C).

Support of the Family is Indispensable

"But for us, this person is not a mere patient with specific depressive symptoms – he/she is family. They suffer, but they do not know what is happening to them: they make others suffer, and everybody feels abandoned because the DSO seems to prefer not to have anything to do with their family. When this occurs, family and friends withdraw, feeling the hurt of rejection. The DSO continues to be sad, unable to define the reason for this. "Carlos Amigo Vallejo in Dolentium Hominum, p.124.

We can't blame the depression on anyone. Remember the 4 C's? *We didn't cause it (depression), we can't cure it, we can't control it; we can only cope with it.* So, the one thing that <u>we can do</u> is have mercy on our DSO and continue learning ways to apply what we have learned about depression at our DEP-ANON meetings. No longer taking responsibility for our loved ones' responsibilities, We share how our Twelve Step DEP -ANON family group has placed emphasis on how we must take care of ourselves. At our DEP-ANON meetings, we see progress, members finding help in other family members, finding confidence and, increased new coping skills.

So often, we have seen how belonging to a group can provide healthy relationships to develop. Our DSO and others consider mutual aid groups essential for emotional healing in the participants, offering change and continued emotional wellness. Being part of a mutual aid group like DEP-ANON is indispensable for the wellbeing of our family life. We are never alone.

The Family is Persistent
in taking care of Itself

"The depressed is not able to make any decision at all. We are face to face with a sad person who has fallen into indifference, one who is personally tired. His life has become an uphill struggle and, freeing himself of it would be a great liberation, a person who spreads pessimism and tiredness, thinks that he is useless and cannot be rehabilitated, is not interested in anything, and walks through the world with anxious hope and enormous, feeling of guilt.

But for us, the person is not a mere patient with specific pathological symptoms. He is our brother we may welcome him and care for him. "

The author points out that when one member of the family suffers, the whole family suffers. He is telling us to take good care of ourselves

"When one of the members is experiencing depression, the family suffers. Attempting to free the depressed person from depression is of little help. They suffer but, they do not know what is happening to them; they make others suffer and, everybody feels betrayed, undefined and, abandoned. The family system is thrown off balance. Family members are conflicted about the DSO's behavior. Conflicts and anger start to flare up - it is true that the family is the best therapist, but they must know that to be **helpful, they must keep focusing on their mental health and wellness.** "

-- Carlos Amigo Villejo, **The Spiritual and Pastoral Care of the Depressed and his Family.** P.142. Dolentium Hominum (Depression). Vatican City, 2004. P.142.

The family will also take to heart and put the Twelve Step spiritual principles into effect as they continue their active participation in DEP-ANON, making every effort to take care of themselves.

Sometimes a family distances themselves from their DSO. They appear to give up on their efforts to pull the DSO out of the pit of depression. It is then that some families seek out help for themselves. This is the most positive move a family can make and a choice that faces the entire family. We will not turn our back on our DSO> We will set up *boundaries* and put *limits* on anything that will cause harm to the DSO or will disrupt the harmony of family life. We will establish *positive practices* that create a stress-free environment for themselves, the DSO, and all in the family. Anything less than this will not work.

Family Support of Depressed Anonymous Meeting for their DSO

The depressed person should form relationships with people who are in recovery and are encouraged to commit themselves to help other people even when they would rather stay in the comfort of their isolation.

(Chapter Ten has as its theme Perseverance. This theme is the potential as a topic for group discussion. Questions follow each of the individual commentaries.)

STEP TEN: PERSEVERANCE
DEP-ANON FAMILY GROUP
DEPRESSED ANONYMOUS - STEP TEN

`STEP TEN: "Continued to take personal inventory and when we were wrong, promptly admitted it."

THEME: PERSEVERANCE

One of the essential lessons that we have learned in this program is not delaying getting into action. Pronto! When we reflect upon our lives, we see how important it is to make a daily inventory examining our day and activities. This summing up lets us know if we have been open and honest with ourselves and ready to let the God of our understanding move in our life. So often, when others are suffering, like our DSO, we naturally want to try and fix them. We think that possibly they will get better (translated – more agreeable to us) so that they can move back into living a normal life. To keep doing the same thing expecting different results is insanity.

We continue to hear how we keep "hands-off" from our depressed family member or friend in the family DEP-ANON group

Often in the group, we hear how other members learn to take care of themselves. We understand that as the focus increases in our own lives that our level of anxiety, feelings of helplessness gradually begin to decrease. Even though we are concerned about the progress, or lack of progress with our DSO, we are discovering that our stress level is gradually lessening.

It is the "miracle of the group" where we begin to heal in this program of recovery, active participants in the DEP-ANON fellowship, seeking that "spiritual awakening" that lets us live in the serenity of doing God's will. Initially, we feel like our car is careening out of control. When this happens, we "white knuckle" the steering wheel, fear freezing us in the moment of panic. But when we loosen our grip, we are willing to let go of our control, and we find ourselves more relaxed and better prepared to be open to the prompting and that small voice of the God of our understanding. Now, granted this relaxing mindset that we need to fix someone, we soon discover that the problem continues to be "us." We learn from our continued work in the group, thinking that curing someone else is an illusion. We have constructed a <u>mental fantasy</u>. If that were all it took to get our DSO freed from the prison of their depression, there would be no need for our DEP-ANON family group or Depressed Anonymous.

The admission and the conviction that it is a surrender of my will where the fellowship, prayer, and daily meditation, alert me to the times I was wrong. I need to move in the direction of making my amends promptly.

The word "promptly" is a keyword in this Step, and it is said this way so we cannot let a festering resentment or hurt become a block to our growth and healing. Our spiritual progress depends on our admission that we need to continue our work on ourselves. We achieve this without fear or anxiousness.

SAMPLE TOPICS/QUESTIONS
FOR GROUP DISCUSSION

1) Do I act "promptly" when and to whom I need to make amends in my life?

2) What can I do to be more forgiving of myself and others? Share what works for you.

3) How has the DEP-ANON fellowship helped me? How have my sponsor and DEP-ANON fellowship helped me take down the blocks that have kept me from growing spiritually?

DO WE HAVE A "CURE" MENTALITY?

Many of us have this "cure" mentality about antidepressants, visits to the psychiatrist, counselors, group therapies. Magic pills and silver bullets play no part in recovery from depression. Our loved one or friend is not acting differently than before. They are taking their meds faithfully but don't seem to be getting better. What is wrong with this picture? We believed that the medicine would bring them around. But no, it's still the same hurting person as before. There is no change. Our hopes begin to slump. We have been kind and patient, we tell ourselves, but that still hasn't turned them around. What's happening here? That is a question many of us have asked. What went wrong?

A Turning Point

Here is our turning point. We struggle with our feelings of being let down. Our DSO is not following our script of recovery. Worst of all, our DSO doesn't seem to care how we feel. They don't understand why we are so disappointed and so frustrated. Indeed, they must hurry and get well - can't they speed up their recovery so that we all can get back to the way life was before their depression hit our family so hard. We all have felt the sudden shock, and yes, we all have hit a brick wall. We find that our lack of control over our DSO proceeds from the same helplessness that the depressed feel. We feel that we have our backs against the wall.

Before our introduction to the fellowship of DEP-ANON, we thought, mistakenly, that we were going to have to increase our efforts to get them well. We had to fix them. And now that has all changed. We can only help ourselves and follow the spiritual principles which continue to demonstrate how we need to take care of ourselves. We can only change ourselves. How can we do that?

Limits and Boundaries

We need to be firm, set limits and, have boundaries for ourselves and our DSO. Any behaviors that threaten the family's well-being will cause severe emotional upsets while simultaneously increasing stress among family members.

Setting limits is a persistent and caring way, plus being a valuable strategy for our families to maintain harmony within the home environment.

The DEP-ANON family has come up with solutions as to how best to protect themselves from the dysfunctional attitudes and behaviors of their DSO. The group's mutuality and their common cause will strengthen support systems for a family that feels it is not causing any positive changes in their DSO's life. It is at this point, as in most other Twelve Step programs of recovery, that those whose solutions are working for one family can provide those same positive results for those family members who are not doing so well.

One pitfall of which we must be aware is that we, like most who have never experienced depression, helpful as that they might feel that their DSO will have a speedy recovery. This expectation gradually leads to further disappointment as the DSO is not making the progress that we had hoped. Are we placing our hopes on our DSO instead of our own needed recovery?

Remember the 4 C's: we didn't cause it, can't cure it, can't control it; only that we can cope with it. These are some of the tools that we are using to gradually detach from needing to take care of someone who needs to take responsibility for themselves, just as we need to take responsibility for ourselves and our mental and emotional health.

Regularly Attending DEP-ANON Meetings

We now know that whether or not our DSO comes to a DA meeting or a support group or not, we will do ourselves a world of good by regularly coming to the DEP-ANON group. You will find members of the fellowship sharing what works for them in the program, plus the strengths they have accumulated by coming to meetings.   In the group, they learn about depression, plus taking care of those areas in their lives with which they need help.

We are learning that I must first take responsibility for myself and my behaviors. Otherwise, all my energies are spent centering on the depressed and worrying about what they need to do. I am learning that I must first take responsibility for my own life and not someone else's. Otherwise, all my energy is going toward the depressed, and my life soon becomes unbalanced and spiraling further down into daily worry and anxiety. And since I place my trust in that Higher Power, I will not let this happen to my DEP-ANON fellowship group and me. I cannot let loose of this life providing investment

(Chapter Eleven has as its theme: Patience. This theme serves as a potential topic for group discussion.

Questions follow each of the individual Step commentaries.)

STEP ELEVEN: PATIENCE
DEP-ANON FAMILY GROUP
DEPRESSED ANONYMOUS - STEP ELEVEN

"Sought through prayer and meditation to improve our conscious contact with God as we understood God, praying only for knowledge of God's will for us and the power to carry it out."

THEME: PATIENCE

Meditation is something that can always be available and further developed. It has no boundaries of width or depth. Aided by such instruction and example as we can find, it is essentially an individual adventure, something which each of us works out in their way. But its object is always the same, to improve our conscious contact with God, with God's grace, wisdom and love.

 Now that we have progressed this far in our program, we know that our recovery is always made more substantial by our group presence.   The more we let go and place our trust in the God of our understanding, a promise is fulfilled, sometimes quickly and other times gradually. We will find less need to keep tabs on whether our DSO is doing what they are supposed to be doing or not doing. Prayer and meditation are the two sides of the same coin, producing for us serenity and daily guidance for living out God's will.

 Just exactly what does "making conscious contact with God" mean? For some, it means making prayer a daily routine and an essential part of one's life. This spiritual discipline of listening to God's inner promptings can, in time, help us believe that we are becoming more in tune with God's promptings, using the spiritual principles of the Twelve Steps. Now that we have spent time making conscious contact with God, we are learning how to gradually listen and seek guidance from the other members of the DEP-ANON group. Discovering God's will for us is what we have found will bring us peace, strength, and hope for our lives. We can go back to Step Three for a little more reflection on this matter. We've already decided to turn over our wills to God. By now, hopefully, this daily practice has become an everyday experience, producing a sense of peace and calmness in our lives. It also helps to have this private time at the same location and at the same time. Habits are made this way, repeating an activity and getting positive results. Habits can be the foundation for character building. After a time, your body clock will alert you to the fact it's prayer and meditation time.

As we continue to mine the wealth of spiritual power in our soul, we begin to realize this as we have a hope of finding more direction from God for a life of serenity, the more there is to discover. The paradox of goodness is that the more good you seek, the more is given to you. What we seek seeks us.   When we spend time in silence waiting to hear God's whisper of hope, our Higher Power manifests its' presence by a powerful feeling of peace. We always want to be sensitive to the pulse of God's love in our hearts.

Meditation can be a powerful "pausing," if you will, "pausing" our mind, thinking and, feelings, bringing ourselves closer toward our authentic self. **A quiet time always gives light!**

We now march to that still small voice of God, prompting us to spend more time listening than talking. Listen closely to your friends at meetings speak about their relationship with   You will hear God's voice more clearly than ever before in your life. You begin to feel that God accompanies each of you to a place where the light of hope and tranquility can become your oasis of joy.

At the DEP-ANON family group meeting, we believe that our efforts with this new way of living and acting are beginning to pay off. Our DSO is a person who has all the tools to work their way out of depression. The family is also continuing their work to walk with their loved ones in mutual respect and love.

It is a paradox that the more we are in contact with God, the less time we spend trying to fix the other this personal effort at taking care of ourselves has a positive effect on our whole family. This powerful drama gradually unfolds into our life as God gently plants "hope-filled thoughts" into our minds, like an attentive gardener. These thoughts are like "seeds," which we nurture along our path and share the fruits with those who need us the most.

This conscious contact helps us be aware of all those old negative thoughts, which, once the familiar and compulsive thoughts, keeping our attention riveted on our DSO instead of on ourselves where it belongs.

Finally, we now believe that it is God's will for each of us to be in touch with God's presence through prayer and meditation. Daily we are learning how to spend meditation time listening for a healing thought from God and members of our group. It is God's will that we stay connected with those people who, like ourselves, are working on a program based on spiritual principles. We want to be conscious of our own needs and those of others as we continue to live with a strong belief that all things are possible with God. Our continued sharing with the DEP-ANON fellowship opens our minds and hearts to the positive individual group testimonies shared during our times together. Our Higher Power continues to manifest itself to each of us in our way, patiently and powerfully.

It takes patience these days to want everything good to happen - yesterday. Today is the day of fast food and drive-through. Make it quick - like now! If we desire that the Higher Power manifest its power in our lives, then we soon learn that our life has to be a keeping an ear open for the gentle prompting of God's Spirit. Most days, God's promptings are like a whisper. Always pay close attention to that still small voice. I highly recommend that each one of us make an effort at keeping a personal journal of God's daily activity in our lives. Choose passages from the Bible or holy writings or Twelve Step literature which especially resonates with your life. You also might choose reflections from the group which came to you during a DEP-ANON meeting and, if so, please write them down for further examination at another time.

One more thought for Step Eleven has to do with the presence of our God at every meeting. At the beginning of my work with Twelve Step programs is how God's presence is manifested so powerfully in our midst. I can often feel the presence of God's Spirit working in our fellowship, accompanying the sharing moments of those members who were especially burdened. I can't attribute the change in my mood in the group meeting to anything but for the attentive listening to those persons surrendering their hearts, minds, and selves to an Almighty and loving God, our Higher Power.

"Came to believe that a power greater than myself could restore me to sanity." STEP TWO

"Patience, that blending of moral courage with physical timidity." - Thomas Hardy

"Possess your soul with patience." - John Dryden

SAMPLE TOPICS/QUESTIONS FOR GROUP DISCUSSION

1) Discuss how prayer and meditation have brought you to a new understanding of yourself and your God? Has the God of your understanding become your Higher Power?

2) Do prayer and meditation help you live with your DSO with more serenity? Share how this works for you.

3) Can you find God's will for yourself more readily now that you are working on a recovery program and being an active participant in the group fellowship?

THE IMPORTANCE OF BELONGING TO A MUTUAL AID GROUP

We are learning how important it is to return week after week to our meetings where we need the courage to continue our focus on ourselves and our recovery. So as not to get "stuck" in the problem, we can talk about a solution and decide how each Step moves us forward for our recovery. Our continued faith relationship with the God of our understanding and the support of our DEP-ANON family group is presenting our lives with hope and trust. DEP-ANON provides us with those solutions needed to put hope back into our lives.

As it says in the Depressed Anonymous book: "There is simply something positive in being part of a mutual aid group and being able to talk about what you are feeling."

Now that our lives no longer have to be played out in the darkness of doubt, we now have a clear vision of the possible change in our thinking and feeling.

Part of the solution for us is to stay out of the mind, thoughts, and feelings of the DSO. We have to let them find their way out of their depression as they work the Steps and continue to take care of themselves physically, emotionally, and spiritually by their frequent attendance at Depressed Anonymous meetings.

Jack Canfield tells us that there are three ways to grow in life: One, quit doing what you have been doing that doesn't work; Two, start doing more of what does work; And Three, start doing things that you've never done before and see if it works."

We are Never Alone!

(Chapter Twelve theme: Charity and Love. This theme serves as a possible topic for group discussion. Questions follow each of the individual Step commentaries.)

STEP TWELVE: CHARITY AND LOVE
DEP-ANON FAMILY GROUP
DEPRESSED ANONYMOUS – STEP TWELVE

STEP TWELVE: "Having had a spiritual awakening as the result of these Steps, we tried to carry the message to those who are still suffering from depression."

THEME: CHARITY AND LOVE

The more I read this Step Twelve, the more I believe that it is the keystone, the arch of that new life that we must pass through to keep that healthy focus on ourselves.

In truth, we know that if someone has been where we have been and then made a decision not to take this powerful message of ours to someone else, we would not be partaking in its healing power today. From what the DEP-ANON family group may say to all new members is that with time and work, they too will be heartened by their being a part of the fellowship of the DEP-ANON Family and Friends of the depressed.

The best ways to stay focused on ourselves is to receive help from our sponsor, each other, the Traditions, and carrying the message of hope to those family members who seek out our assistance and experience.

Most of us have gone through those frustrations where we all have felt hopeless and restricted being around the depressed family member. We all have thought that we could motivate them the more we told them what they needed to do to escape from the rigors of depression. Paradoxically, this just seemed to intensify their resistance to change. For many of us who have never been depressed ourselves, it is to make the mistake that many family members make with their DSO. The more we push the depressed, attempting to get them motivated, the less motivated they become. I think there is a lesson here. And that is what we all have found, and that it is necessary to set up a DEP-ANON family group, using our Twelve Steps as guides and principles for living. It just makes a lot of sense to get a group established where others like ourselves can gather and support each other.

We must learn how to take care of ourselves if we are to be supportive of a family member. There has to be a seismic shift in how we treat ourselves. That has been the message we have received since joining the DEP-ANON family group.

The spiritual awakening that grows inside of each of us provides not only a relief for ourselves but for all those family members who are looking for the best ways to help themselves while indirectly helping their DSO.

The hope we experience today and every day that we have a group of loving people who are all going through the same challenges.

One thing to remember is that we are a very precious resource providing our experiences with each other giving us support and guidance. We also plan to continue our practice of helping all group members learn about depression and the physical and mental effects on the one depressed, plus all their family members and friends.

When we let God take charge, it is at this time that we find a more excellent happening than when we first sought God's help and guidance.

We learn by studying the Steps, the support we receive from each other, the witness of our fellowship through sharing our strengths, hope, and experiences. We begin to see the light. And as often as we come together as a fellowship, we are most aware of how the God of our understanding guides us every step of the way. Bill W., the co-founder of AA, tells us how it becomes plain that "the group must survive or the individual will not."

SAMPLE TOPICS/QUESTIONS
FOR GROUP DISCUSSION

1) Please share with the group what part DEP-ANON is having in your life today? Please share with the group an example.

2) How important is the DEP-ANON message that we need to take care of ourselves first? Please share your thoughts.

3) How has your understanding of the nature of depression helped you feel differently about your DSO? Please give some examples.

4) Do you agree that our DSO has a mutual aid program developed by others who will find kindred spirits to help them find serenity and spontaneity from recovering a purpose and meaning for their lives?

APPENDIX A

How to relate to someone who is depressed?

It is most tempting to find out someone is depressed to immediately fix the problem. The following responses are more likely to help.

The things that didn't make me feel worse are words which 1) **acknowledge my depression for what it is.** ("No, it's just a phase." Not helpful.) 2) **Permit me to feel depressed** ("But why should you be sad?" Not helpful.)

Here is a list of the **best** *things that will be most helpful to a depressed friend.*

I love you.
I care.
You are not alone in this.
I am not going to leave you or abandon you.
Do you want a hug?
It will pass; we can ride it out together.
When this is all over, I'll still be here (If you mean it), and so will you.
Don't say anything - just be here.
Hey, you're not crazy.
May the strength of the past reflect in your future.
God does not play dice with the universe (Albert Einstein).
A miracle is simply a do-it-yourself project (S. Leek).
We are not simply on earth to see through one another but to see someone through.
I understand your pain, and I empathize with you.

I am sorry that you are in such pain. I am not going to leave you.
I listen to you talk about it, and I can't imagine what it's like for you.
I can't fully understand what you are feeling, but I can offer my compassion and presence.
You are important to me. If you need a friend, give me a call. (And mean it).
Source: Compiled by bw@cv.hp.com Version 12. April 29, 1995, via WWW

The *worst* things to say to someone who is depressed are the following comments.

It's all in your mind.
Pull yourself up by your bootstraps.
You have so many things to be thankful for; why are you depressed?
You have it so good; why aren't you happy?
Well, at least it's not that bad.
There are a lot of people worse off than you.
Have you got tired of all this "me-me" stuff?
Everybody has a bad day now and then.
You can do anything you want if you just set your mind to it.
You don't look depressed.
Source: Compiled bw@cv.hp.com at
http://www.exccpe.com/corbeau/worst.html

APPENDIX B

THE 12 STEPS OF DEP-ANON

1) We admitted that we were powerless over our depressed loved one - that our lives had become unmanageable.
2) We came to believe that a Power greater than ourselves could restore us to sanity.
3) We made a decision to turn our will and our lives over to the care of God as we understood God.
4) We made a searching and fearless moral inventory of ourselves.
5) We admitted to God, to ourselves, and to another human being the exact nature of our wrongs.
6) We were entirely ready to have God remove all these defects of character.
7) We humbly asked God to remove our shortcomings.
8) We made a list of all persons who we had harmed and became willing to make amends to them all.
9) We made direct amends to such people wherever possible, except when to do so would injure them or others.
10) Continued to take a personal inventory when we were wrong, promptly admitted it.
!!) Sought through prayer and meditation to improve our conscious contact with God as we understood God, praying only for knowledge of God's will for us and the power to carry it out.

12) Having had a spiritual awakening as the result of these Steps, we tried to carry the message to the depressed family member and others practicing these principles in all of our affairs.

THE TWELVE TRADITIONS OF DEP-ANON

1) Our common welfare should come first; personal progress depends upon DEP-ANON unity.
2) For our group purpose, there is but one ultimate authority – a loving God who may express itself in our group conscience. Our leaders are but trusted servants; they do not govern.
3) The only requirement for our DEP-ANON fellowship is for family members and friends to have a relative or friend who is suffering from depression.
4) Each group should be autonomous except in matters affecting the DEP-ANON group or other DEP-ANON groups.
5) Each DEP-ANON group has but one primary purpose - to support those family members and friends of the depressed. We do this using the Twelve Steps of DEP-ANON and inform ourselves on the nature of depression and focus on our physical, spiritual and, mental well-being. We cannot fix our depressed loved ones.
6) A DEP-ANON group should never endorse, finance, or lend the DEP-ANON name to any related facility or outside enterprise, lest

problems of money, property, and prestige divert us from our primary purpose.

7) Every DEP-ANON group ought to be fully self-supporting, declining outside contributions.

8) DEP-ANON should remain forever non-professional, but our service centers may employ special workers.

9) DEP-ANON ought never to be organized, but we may create service boards or committees directly responsible to those they serve.

10)   DEP-ANON has no opinion on outside issues; hence the DEP-ANON name ought never to be drawn into public controversy.

11)   Our public relations policy is based on attraction rather than promotion. We need always to maintain personal anonymity at the level of press, radio, and films.

12)   Anonymity is the spiritual foundation of our traditions, ever reminding us to place principles before personalities.

APPENDIX C

TOOLS OF RECOVERY

TOPICS FOR GROUP STEP MEETINGS DISCUSSIONS AND PERSONAL REFLECTION

CUT OFF NEGATIVE THINKING/ ENABLE POSITIVE THINKING/ "SUNSPOTS" AND THE "LAW OF THE THREES."

When you have a negative image or thought which produces unpleasant feelings, replace it immediately with three positive and pleasant thoughts or mental images. We call this **THE LAW OF THE THREES.** One negative thought is immediately replaced by three pleasant thoughts or/and memories. As a group member, you and the group might want to spend some time-sharing positive images of yourselves, doing activities promoting the care of yourself since the last gathering. These positive images of yourself, putting your recovery first, will each group member present.

SUNSPOTS are some of your past happy memories that come easily pictured in your mind. When we are in that mood of deep despair, and all seems hopeless, it is a good practice to bring out your mental album of happy memories and reflect on them - taking time to experience those same positive emotions that accompanied those images at that time.

We page through many pictures in our albums, and one or two or more will bring a new emotion, hopefully, a happy one, into the present moment.

The results of these two behaviors, **SUNSPOTS** and

THE LAW OF THE THREES, and talking about them with the group will resonate with them and their own lives.

POSITIVE SELF-TALK

Negative self-talk can send you into a downward spiral quickly. It is vitally important to start negative self-talk to replace it with positive self-talk. Physically divert your thinking, take a walk, go outside, listen to your favorite music, walk a dog. Call a member on the phone or email them. Go to an online 12 Step meeting at ZOOM or SKYPE and share your feelings there.

PRAYER

Speaking to the God of your understanding can bring you peace that you might not have experienced before in your life. Prayer is the lifeblood of our program of recovery. Through prayer and meditation, we can draw closer to the infinite being who we call God and who will be part of that guiding spirit accompanying us through every minute of our lives.

Prayer will **Improve** our conscious contact with the God of our understanding. You can't go wrong when you surrender to the power that created the universe and created you with your uniqueness and God's mysterious presence in your heart and mind.

JOURNALING PRODUCES THOUGHT CLARIFICATION

This simple act of writing something down is helpful because to do so, as we have to bring to mind a special thought or emotion, pleasant or unpleasant, with its special feeling attached to it. Journaling helps us deal with all those emotions tumbling around in our minds. We write these feelings down and see them in black and white letters causing our lives so much pain and confusion. Many times, it may seem like untying knots.

Now we can look at what we have written and, instead of a loose thought falling into a world that only existed a few seconds before, we can come to a better resolution on what form of action we should take. This is recovery

By journaling, I make every effort to get in touch with who I am. I am taking the opportunity now to focus on what gets me down and what keeps me up. Writing thoughts and feelings down on paper lets me look more deeply at what has been going on in my life just for these past 24 hours.

So, get your notebook, mark the date of your writing and then have some reflections, writing down the major mood(s) that you experienced today. Other members of the DEP-ANON find writing down their answers to the Depressed Anonymous Workbook a beneficial journaling practice.

SOCIAL ENGAGEMENT

No man or woman or child is an island. Emotional isolation, fueled by feelings of fear and anxiety that accompanies it leaves us prone to feelings of depression.

As humans, we need others; we love being with others. It's in our DNA to be social creatures. But we are also aware of the problems that can exist when we begin to isolate ourselves, withdraw and stay cooped up in prison we have unwittingly created.

In our present situation of the Covid-19 pandemic, we have the government mandate to social distance from each other (six feet apart).   Social ties in normal times provided us health and togetherness. Isolation creates some real problems. Isolation can be a potential risk to our physical health and mental health.

Those of us who are members of the DEP-ANON fellowship have come together to support each other. Talking to a friend or attending a 12 step DEP-ANON Family meeting and the strength that comes from these encounters ensures greater strength and help for ourselves and each other. Our group meetings will lift our spirits, elevate our mood and inspire us to work on our recovery alongside those others in our fellowship.

EXERCISE

Choose a physical activity that you may enjoy. Walking is the easiest and one of the best that you can do regularly. Frequency is more important than how much time is afforded to any activity. Some Doctors in the UK now write out prescriptions for depressed patients to walk so many times a week.

I can see family members doing joint activities which are physically healthy and emotionally supportive.

Possibly a hiking club could be formed for those in the DEP-ANON Family and Friends Group.

BEING IN NATURE

Surrounding yourself in nature, away from the noise and stress of urban life, can have a soothing and calming effect on the human spirit.

I found walking around the beautiful grounds of a Franciscan monastery provided me with moments of peace and hope amid a hundred acres of wooded forest. The lake was calm and looked like a sheet of sparkling blue water with diamond-like sprouts shooting up over the lake's surface. A few years back, I spent three days alone, next to a lake inlet. To my surprise, I could be a part of the natural environment where the hummingbirds, turtles, and assorted life surrounded me. It was just God, me, and God's amazing creatures, all part of a dynamic panoramic. No radio, no TV, no phone,

Working out solutions for our mental health and serenity, the beauty of nature gives us a respite from worry and those negative thoughts that keep churning around in our minds. So, get up, move around and let the natural world remind us how everything that lives and breathes is part of everything else that breaths.

Be in the center of creation with its beautiful diversity - including every kind of living creation, the trees, wildlife, and all nature's beauty. There is abundant activity all around us, directing our seeing, hearing, and smell from our inner world of pain. As a family member with a depressed loved one, it is an absolute necessity to focus on the beauty surrounding surrounds us. We have to go and be part of it.

I believe that just moving the body in the world of nature will ignite a hope that life has to get better. So, get up, get out of yourself and find a world, a wonderful world full of life, beauty, and hope. It will serve you well.

MINDFULNESS/STAYING IN THE PRESENT

Staying in the present is a simple and effective way to keep your mind focused on the present, observing your thoughts and experiences as they occur without judgment. By keeping the focus "on the moment," it is possible to acknowledge the source of your stress without dwelling on it or attaching too much meaning to it.

Practicing mindfulness helps you reserve judgment on the accuracy of your thoughts and feelings and observe them for what they are – products of your mind.

Here are the basic steps to follow when practicing mindfulness.

1) Focus on your breathing or some other sensation or an object in your surroundings. It could be a beautiful flower or a part of your natural environment.

2) While focusing, allow other thoughts and feelings to flow over you. Let them pass before the mind screen, like watching a bus move slowly down the street. Remember not to get on.

3) Acknowledge and name each feeling and then let it fade away. Allow the next thought or feeling to enter your mind. Again, acknowledge it, and then let it go.

4) When learning mindfulness, individuals are encouraged to practice 30 minutes a day to

become comfortable with this practice. Also, sit in a comfortable chair or space, let this practice be part of your daily meditation time, and do it every day, preferably at the same time every day. This daily practice can help form a habit of automatically setting up a bodily slowdown.

5) Stay in the present. "Do not dwell in the past, do not dream of the future; concentrate your mind on the present moment. Be in the now." Like negative thinking, catch yourself as quickly as possible and refocus on the task at hand and continue to stay in the present moment.

6) Today is all that we have. Don't let dwelling on yesterday's hurts and fears or about tomorrow rob you of your peace today. You are responsible for how you think and feel.

7) Through your prayer and meditation time, you can be lifted and know that a Power greater than yourself is guiding you on this road of recovery – one day at a time. As a member of a 12-Step program of recovery, DEP-ANON, we believe in a Higher Power, something greater than ourselves. God provides strength and comfort to us when we pray and hope for our healing, particularly that of our family member who is depressed.

8) The best way to live today is to be fully conscious of the present moment and create for yourself that strong desire to be part of it. Let's not live in yesterday – the rent might kill us. Just still your mind and body and relax part of your body, starting with your feet, working your mind's eye up to the crown of your head. Talk to

yourself, telling your body areas to "just relax" as you spend a bit of time with each part, then move on. Don't worry about time.

SLEEPING

Sleeping is one of the best things you can do for your health. Sleep keeps the immune system strong and healthy and reduces daily stressors. Talk to a doctor about how much sleep a person your age needs. Other DEP-ANON members can share with you how they get a good night's sleep. Those who are older might find that a nap in the after-lunch hour can provide them with energy for the remainder of their day.

NUTRITION

Discover the foods that are good for you, for your metabolism. These are fruits, vegetables, fish, poultry, and salads. Find a balanced food plan instead of eating food that will cause extra weight to build up in our arteries and heart. Stay away from sugar. Follow the federal guidelines for a healthy diet. If you don't have a food plan for yourself now, please develop one for your health and happiness. Remember, stress will push you to cram your bodies with nutrition less foods, like chips and sugar, which can damage your immune system plus raise your blood pressure. Please examine your eating habits – they do have consequences.

APPENDIX D

SUGGESTED DEP-ANON FAMILY GROUP MEETING FORMAT

LEADERS AND DISCUSSION MEETING GUIDE FOR FAMILY AND FRIENDS OF THE DEPRESSED.

The Chair reads the following to open the meeting:

Hello, my name is_____. I want to welcome you to the fellowship of **DEP-ANON**, a group meeting where persons can come together to find strength, hope, and acceptance. And just as our loved ones can participate in their fellowship of Depressed Anonymous, we now have a program and fellowship where we will learn how to live with the depressed. We will also learn more about the depression experience and focus on our lives. We gather here for a common purpose, to focus on our recovery, emotionally and spiritually. We can do this best by participating in our **DEP-ANON** group fellowship.

DEP-ANON is a mutual aid group where persons with similar needs can generate positive energies, form friendships and give each other the strength to live each new day with hope. We are a Twelve Step program of recovery that is not professionally led and is self-supporting.

The Chair OPENS THE MEETING WITH A MOMENT OF SILENCE.

ALL SAY THE SERENITY PRAYER

"God grant me the serenity to accept the things I cannot change, the courage to change the things I can, and the wisdom to know the difference."

Chair or Volunteer reads the **DEP-ANON STATEMENT OF CONCERN.**

Points to remember

1) We rely upon the Twelve Steps and Twelve Traditions of the DEP-ANON Family and Friends group for knowledge and wisdom.

2) The Twelve Steps and Traditions are the principles and guides for developing honest and fulfilling relationships with ourselves, our depressed family members, and friends.

3) This renewal process is a gift of healing for us. By actively working the program of **DEP-ANON**, we can achieve a new peace, a release from our efforts to try and change others and to put some joy in our lives.

4) **DEP-ANON** is neither a **medical group nor a religious** group, so any discussion of medications or religious dogma is out of place here.

Leader or Volunteer reads the following.

5) **DEP-ANON** is not a replacement for an individual's relationship with his or her therapist.

6) **Crosstalk** occurs when the group member interrupts a person who has the floor. We do not offer any advice to those who speak. We also share in terms of "I," not "you," and only share how the Step or floor discussion is affecting me

personally. When a member of the group is recognized to speak, they share only that which affects them. Each person is allowed only 3-5 minutes a share. Questions which arise during the meeting can be raised after the meeting.

    7) **Anonymity** is not just a question of our name. It's an essential element in our recovery. It is helpful for family members to feel that they can come forward without revealing their identity. Perhaps even more importantly, anonymity stresses the unity of **DEP-ANON**, which depends on the acceptance that we are all equal in the fellowship. **Anonymity reminds us to place principle above personality in this program of spiritual growth and healing.**

We ask that:

WHOM YOU SEE HERE
WHAT YOU HEAR HERE,
WHEN YOU LEAVE HERE,
LET IT STAY HERE!

<u>Leader</u> welcomes the newcomers.
<u>Volunteer</u> reads the following (See Appendix B)
12 Steps of DEP-ANON
12 Traditions of DEP-ANON
DISCUSSION MEETING OR STEP MEETING (To be decided by group fellowship).

DISCUSSION TIME

A Meeting can be a Topic or, Step meeting to be decided by members or, the <u>Leader</u> can suggest a topic for discussion.

<u>Leader:</u> Opens up the meeting for the Group discussion time.

The Leader indicates that if this is a Topic Meeting, a member or meeting Leader can suggest a topic for discussion.

If this is a Step Meeting, members will share their hope, strengths, and experiences, applying a Step that they have used this past week in their personal life.

All of the DEP-ANON Steps, each with their commentary, have attached questions used for group discussions.

The TOOLS OF RECOVERY (See Appendix A) can also serve as Topics for discussion.

The <u>Leader</u> closes the meeting.

The <u>Leader</u> gives each member a chance to say what they hope to do positively for themselves until the next meeting time. Each member can comment briefly on one hopeful or helpful statement which particularly struck them at the meeting.

PASS THE BASKET: The Leader asks for a donation from those who can put something in the basket to pay for group needs. Each group is self-supporting. (Tradition Seven of DEP-ANON)

The Leader asks for a volunteer for the next meeting time.

Final Prayer (Our Father or Serenity Prayer)

"God, grant me the serenity to accept the things I cannot change, the courage to change the things I can, and the wisdom to know the difference."

BIBLIOGRAPHY

Al-Anon Works for Families and Friends of the Alcoholic. Al-Anon Book Groups. 20008.

Alcoholics Anonymous: The Story of how Men and Women have Recovered from Alcoholism. Alcoholics Anonymous, World Services. NY.NY.1955.

As Bill Sees it. The A.A. Way of Life. Selected Writings of A.A Co-Founder, Alcoholics Anonymous World Services, Inc. NY.NY. 1955.

Twelve Steps and Twelve Traditions. Alcoholics Anonymous World Services, Inc. New York, NY/1981.

Depressed Anonymous: The Story of Men and Women Who Have Recovered from Depression. Third Edition. Depressed Anonymous Publications. Louisville. KY. 1990, 2008, 2011.

Hugh Smith Depressed? Here is a Way Out! Fount, UK. 1990.

Dorothy Rowe, Depression: The Way out of Your Prison. Routledge, Kegan and Paul. London.1963, 1996. Second Edition. Published by Routledge.

Jorge Enrique Iminez Carvajal. The Role of the Family Faced with Depression. Pp. 140I. In Dolentium Hominum. No. 55--Year xix. No.1 2004. Journal of the

Pontifical Council for Health Pastoral Care. Proceedings of the XVIII International Conference Organized by the Pontifical Council for Health Pastoral Care. DEPRESSION. November 13-14-15, 2003. Vatican City.

Carlos Amigo Vallejo. The Spiritual and Pastoral Care of the Depressed Person and the Family. In Dolentium Hominum, pp. 142-144.

Shel Silverstein. The Missing Piece. (Children's Picture book). HarperCollins. 1976.

Made in the USA
Monee, IL
08 July 2021